How will you spend your summjue,
we're invited to reflect on First ... :ould
be a good way to oil your think ...
*Julia Cameron, writer, editor and* ... rmation
Walking Tour

I've been travelling internationally for forty-five years. I wish I'd been able
to read this book a long time ago – it would certainly have made me travel
more thoughtfully. This is a travelogue, it's theology, it's cultural education
and it's a challenge to undertake mission all rolled into one. A fascinating read.
*Peter Maiden, International Director Emeritus, Operation Mobilisation and
former Chairman, Keswick Ministries*

This book reminds us that everything is theological. What a marvellous
journey through the stories of Scripture (and the author's life); it will
challenge, encourage and widen your perspective, not only on travel
but also on the amazing One who created everything. In a world where
it's easier than ever to work or study abroad, this book deserves to be
widely read.
*Sinead Norman, International Fellowship of Evangelical Students*

We all have twenty-four hours a day available to us, but how do we decide
how to use that time for the best? Peter Grier gives us excellent fresh ideas
for honouring God with our travels, and helps to shape perspectives on
mission, tourism and the meaningful welcoming of overseas students.
*Alan Tower, National Director, Friends International*

# TRAVEL

12 APR 1985

To London

ivp

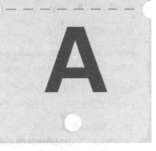

AIRLINE BAGGAGE

SORTING

# TRAVEL

IN TANDEM WITH GOD'S HEART

PETER GRIER

INTER-VARSITY PRESS
36 Causton Street, London SW1P 4ST, England
Email: ivp@ivpbooks.com
Website: www.ivpbooks.com

First published 2018

**British Library Cataloguing-in-Publication Data**
A catalogue record for this book is available from the British Library.

ISBN: 978–1–78359–735–2
eBook ISBN: 978–1–78359–736–9

Set in Myriad 11/15 pt
Typeset in Great Britain by CRB Associates, Potterhanworth, Lincolnshire
Printed in Great Britain by Ashford Colour Press Ltd, Gosport, Hampshire

*Inter-Varsity Press publishes Christian books that are true to the Bible and that
communicate the gospel, develop discipleship and strengthen the church for its
mission in the world.*

*IVP originated within the Inter-Varsity Fellowship, now the Universities and
Colleges Christian Fellowship, a student movement connecting Christian Unions
in universities and colleges throughout Great Britain, and a member movement
of the International Fellowship of Evangelical Students. Website: www.uccf.org.uk.
That historic association is maintained, and all senior IVP staff and committee
members subscribe to the UCCF Basis of Faith.*

# CONTENTS

# ACKNOWLEDGMENTS

Having been brought up in a bookselling family, I knew what it was to devour books, sell books, own books and talk about books, but little did I ever think I would walk in my grandad's footsteps and actually write a book myself.

Despite benefiting from a culture of reading, I don't think I ever appreciated all that went into writing a book – the years of thought and talking with people, the months of writing, the editing, the feedback, the design, the marketing. And so, it's the community of people that have made this book possible that I want to acknowledge at the outset.

Most directly, I want to thank the whole team at IVP UK for even allowing me this opportunity, and especially Senior Commissioning Editor Eleanor Trotter who has been so patient with me as a first-time author. But I also want to thank all those working behind the scenes helping me to bring this book into existence.

My sincere thanks to all who read the drafts at various stages and gave feedback, particularly my parents who spent long hours offering helpful review and discussion. But also huge thanks to all those who shaped my theology and life, from those who preached God's word faithfully for many years, to those who today mentor me, meet me regularly to keep me accountable, and those in Christian Unions Ireland and the wider IFES family who have provided time and space for me to learn from some of the finest Christian thinkers.

To those student travellers from Christian Unions across Munster who inspired me to think about this topic and have given me hours of pleasure as we've discussed God's world together and sought to live out his purposes in it – thank you!

For the record, let me say that most names in the stories that follow have been changed, and many of the details have been amended to spare people's blushes. There have been many other ideas, stories and themes that you have brought to my attention, which I regret I could not include, and so I must acknowledge the limited focus of this book, even within a theology of travel, as we confine ourselves in the main to the theme of pleasure travel. For other travel themes, other resources written and as yet unwritten will have to be your guide: some of you will already have contributed, and will continue to contribute, to my blog <https://aljabr7.wordpress.com/book/>.

Finally, let me admit that any unintentional errors and false emphases will indeed have to be mine, as I've sought how best to reflect what God in his grace has revealed to us in his word.

May we enjoy all that God has given us as we travel onwards.

With love and prayers
Peter Grier, Cork
June 2018

## INTRODUCTION
## #WANDERLUST

The universe is a sort of book, whose first page one has read
when one has seen only one's own country.
(Louis-Charles Fougeret de Monbron)[1]

The only true voyage of discovery, the only fountain
of Eternal Youth, would be not to visit strange lands but to
possess other eyes, to behold the universe through the eyes
of another, of a hundred others, to behold the hundred
universes that each of them beholds, that each of them is.
(Marcel Proust)[2]

**Destination**: A golden beach, western Morocco
**Weather**: 30 degrees, blue skies and a gentle breeze
**Company**: Three Aussies

'Freedom at last!' I thought as I lay back on my towel, soaking in
every degree of the Moroccan summer sun. Ironically, the texts

that I was getting from back home (on the one occasion when I bothered to turn on my phone) said that summer had hit my native Ireland too. Typical!

Somewhat unusually for me, I was the only one left lazing around, as the others had gone off to paddleboard across the blue lagoon. Today, unlike most days where I wouldn't have been content to lie down for over fifteen minutes for fear of missing a potential adventure, I was in no rush. As I lay back in the sun, the sounds of giggling wafted across the water, followed by a splash as my friends tried to push each other off their paddleboards.

Brian and Jo were two Australian medics, in the UK for two years to help the burgeoning National Health Service (NHS) cope with increased demand. While in Europe it was an ideal time for them to escape those nasty hours of shiftwork and explore another side of the world, previously unseen. From cliff-jumping in Malta, to tasting the delights of Mediterranean food and ice cream in Italy and driving Ireland's own Wild Atlantic Way, they were falling in love with their Creator over and over again and being blown away by his amazing world.

Next to them on the paddleboards was their friend Annabel who had left a top Australian job to do missionary work among a people group where God's name was not yet known,[3] normally living these days in a rural, sub-Saharan village in Africa. She had no running water near her mud hut, no electricity and very little local language. To add to her hardships, the 45-degree desert sun made many hours of the day unbearable, and she didn't get on with her multicultural team all that well. Food arrived every fortnight from a market stall in a town miles away. For two days they could eat fruit and meat. After that all that could survive the heat were onions, spices, pasta and rice. At every meal. And if that wasn't bad enough, Boko Haram[4] were reportedly only a few hours down the road, week by week raiding villages, pillaging, raping and killing. Each week her team wondered: would this be the week when they would die for Jesus?

And then there was me. A twenty-something-year-old millennial wondering what to do with my life, paralysed by choice, while currently working to support and disciple Christians in Irish universities and colleges. And with very short college terms, long hours of work (to compensate), and a lot of time on the road from city to city, I was weary for a break by the end of every term, well away from the roads I travelled each week.

What a random bunch of us! But in the intensity of our work settings, we were glad to be away together, particularly Annabel, who couldn't holiday alone in any country near her, as a lone female in such a cultural context wouldn't be appropriate.

The beach was ours to enjoy, with not another Westerner in sight. And soon I had my eyes closed, so very far away from the 24/7 rush and busy life back home. The relentless, crashing waves on the other side of the dune made for a soothing backing track as I drifted off. We had found our untouched paradise.

I was awoken a short while later as three wet bundles landed themselves, still giggling away, on to their towels beside me, making sure to splash whatever water they could in my direction.

Having watched our little posse of joy, all now quite tired from the activities of the morning, lie down, a fourth voice soon joined their conversation, alternating between Arabic, French and English, as he tried to fathom why he couldn't quite piece where we were from.

Salaam, my friends! You are very welcome to this town. The water is beautiful, no? Ask me anything and I can get it for you. Are you hungry and want some food? Perhaps I can cook you some freshly caught crab, just where you are here?

And after a bit of chat, and sensing a business opportunity, he was off to the rock pools nearby, soon to return with a giant crab, bigger than I'd ever seen before, still wriggling to escape his clutches. With the question of its being Ramadan[5] in my head, when public eating and drinking are often not allowed, we politely declined, unsure whether we'd really made the right decision. After saying our goodbyes, and as the others rested or read, the soothing rhythms of the crashing waves ensued, and I was again alone with my thoughts.

How could we make the most of our travels? We were all travellers, and not just on this holiday.

Two enthralled by the pleasures of seeing Europe. One adventuring for the risk of sharing the gospel where Christ is not known. And me, mundanely filling tank after tank of petrol to traverse the same roads each week between universities, in a relatively routine job.

Which takes me back to where it all started. And I have to warn you, it didn't seem like an auspicious start at all . . .

A few months earlier I had broken down in tears in the middle of a car journey. I was travelling the usual two-hour trip to another campus to support a particularly struggling Christian group of students (a Christian Union or 'CU'), and I'd got a text from one of them, yet again: 'Don't think we'll have CU this week, Peter. We'll go bowling instead.'

Regularly, there was something else to prevent God's word being opened and Jesus being made known. And the texts often came last minute, which meant I was already on the road, having made hours of preparation for the meeting. It was a time when, through the tears and the bitterness, I eventually – it took a while and God was patient through several years of driving – came to think how I could use this travel time for his glory, instead of seeing it as wasted. And that made me question further: what does God think of travel as a whole?

It was a question that nagged at me each week for many weeks, as in every university I went to I would meet students who would ask me four questions. Well, three questions really and a statement:

'Who are you?'
'What are you studying?'
'The weather's been all right this week, hasn't it?'
    (Statement, not a question.)
'Were you away anywhere nice over the holidays?'
    Or, failing that, 'Where do you want to go next?'

The travel bug had hit Ireland! (But it will still never replace the weather as the most-talked-about conversation topic.) Though it wasn't just in conversation that this was happening.

On my Instagram feed, stunning imagery from around the world would pop up, sent from travelling students 24/7. Or coming from young professionals behind their desks, yearning for the time they would be free, on their coveted annual leave and re-posting the best of memories. Or even coming from young parents secretly longing already for the day when they'd be free of parenting to go travelling again!

Even in my work and city I would be reminded of travel as thousands of international students would cram into lecture halls each semester, only to be replaced in equal number by ones with similar-sounding names and backgrounds a year or even a semester later. 'Where are the best places to travel in Ireland, Peter?' they would quiz me.

And at the other end of the island, from within the four walls of the family home that I'd grown up in, in a small suburb of a monocultural community still split and hurting from recent political history, one of my sisters married a Pacific Islander and now lives in sub-Saharan Africa with him; another married an Englishman and they now live in a sprawling urban setting filled with too many nationalities to name. And then there's me in Cork, a small Irish city. Well, for now, anyway.

'The world is your oyster,' they told me upon entering university. And this could never be truer, for many. Go anywhere, do anything. Be whoever you want to be. Beautifully freeing. Or paralysing, depending on which way you want to look at it.

My great-grandparents headed off to Manchuria in China to be missionaries, and that was radical indeed for those days. If you went on that long-haul boat trip for months, you rarely came back. And for my great-grandparents to choose their career was also a novelty for their generation, as they were expected to follow a family trade. As for my parents, they started to network sufficiently widely for Dad even to travel six hours down the road to Mum on the other end of the island when they were courting. Life is very different now, and things have changed relatively quickly. Remember, it was only the 1990s that brought cheap air travel that enabled even relatively poor people to traverse the globe.

But with such fast change, not everyone is happy with this relatively new travel bug that has hit our shores.

> 'Running off to Spain and then shouting about it on social media with photo after photo – it's so self-centred!'
> *A 28-year-old married man in Cork*

> 'Peter, how can I get my son to care for the traditional ties of loving his family and neighbours? He's off making friends on the other side of the world.'
> *A worried mum, whose brother is regularly in hospital in Oxford*

> 'Back in my day if we travelled it was on mission trips. Now young people just amuse themselves on holiday. Don't they know there's a dying world out there?'
> *A disgusted grandparent in Belfast*

It wasn't just the parents of my housemate Dan, who had decided to cycle home from New Zealand to Ireland over the course of a year, who were on the phone to me to question this craze. Nor the worried parents whose daughter went off to Laos to smuggle Bibles. I've had remarks from all sorts of people who want me to stop their student friends and family from travelling. And it's not always the older generation either.

And faced with this situation, these reactions and the tug of travelling on my own heart, I'm left thinking: 'Are the above valid comments to make and questions to raise? And are we really making the most of our travels?'

If you're anything like me, you'll have your own gut instincts. Or, perhaps more than that, you'll know exactly how everyone else should be making the most of their lives and travels! But regardless, those instincts will have been shaped by many things: your family background and class; the part of the world you grew up in; when in world history you are living; your local culture; your experiences so far in life; and ultimately, hopefully, your world view or theology. These are all lenses through which we see the world.

So, before we rush to answer the questions above, I want you to join me on a travel journey of our own in the coming chapters. It's a journey that will encompass much of the globe, where we'll experience many cultures. But more than just expanding our horizons, it's a journey that will help us to see beyond our view to a 360-degree panorama.

God's panorama.

A grand panorama of travel, richer than we could ever imagine, which will enhance our tiny glimpse of the world and make sense of it. We'll be taking the journey from Genesis to Revelation like never before, stopping off at our favourite spots along the way, and moving more quickly through others. It's a journey that in some ways will have no end, even after these pages have long run out. But don't worry about that for now.

Finding the right travel partner is harder than you might imagine, but you may wish to pick a fellow 'traveller' with whom to read this, and help each other to reflect on the questions at the end of each chapter. If you're brave, pick someone who doesn't think like you, or someone who'd never leave their front door, and learn from each other as you travel together. And if you don't object, I've even invited along a few friends who'll join us for parts of the journey too. I'll introduce you to them as we go along.

But for now, let's saddle up, because there are quite a few hours of sunlight left today.

**Questions for the road**
- What's top of your bucket list?
- What lenses do you look through as you view the world?
- Where on the spectrum do you find yourself: travelling and enjoying the world, or wanting to hold back from that kind of life?
- How do you think your lenses influence your answers?

Pray that God would help us to see his heart for travel, look through his lenses and learn more as we journey together.

### Prayer

Loving, heavenly Father,
we praise you, the great Creator God,
who made all of this earth;
we're excited to explore it and to plumb the depths
of the good things you have given us.
But even more, we're excited to know you because you
will be infinitely better than your creation.
We'd love to know your heart for this world,
how you see it.
And so, we ask you to teach us.
You see everything, across all time, but our vision
is limited to our culture, our short history,
our limited learning and our experiences.
So, we come and confess that we need you if we are
going to make the most of our travels and of this world.
Would you lead us and guide us as we journey together?
In your Son's name,
Amen.

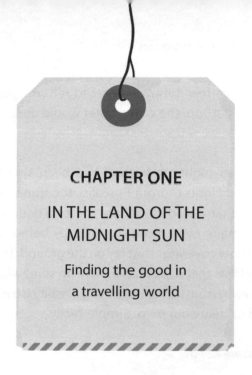

## CHAPTER ONE

## IN THE LAND OF THE MIDNIGHT SUN

### Finding the good in a travelling world

Not all those who wander are lost.
(J. R. R. Tolkien)[1]

**Destination**: The Arctic Circle, Norway
**Weather**: 4 degrees, blue skies
**Company**: One Norwegian, one Irishwoman

'And *what* age were you when that happened?!' roared our Norwegian friend, trying not to laugh too much, as I nervously looked round to see how many in the café were listening.

'Only twenty-five,' came my reply, trying to look shamefaced, but secretly rather proud of our activities.

I was half-way through telling her about our 'Northern Lights' experience in Ireland, but I feared my story might just have been sidetracked for a few minutes never to return again, as every time I tried to start up, she or my sister would descend into a fit of giggles.

Our dark winter nights in Ireland had been spent dreaming of the Northern Lights (Aurora Borealis), the stunning display of natural lights that would illuminate the long dark nights in the Arctic, often made even more dramatic by being reflected off the perfect snow coverings that lay on the ground. There weren't many bucket lists that didn't have them on somewhere. And so, many miles away from it ever becoming a reality (so we thought), we decided to create our own. Simple, really.

So, what did we need?

1. One YouTube video.
2. One projector.
3. One large sheet.
4. One set of fairy lights.
5. One chill-out/electronic music playlist.

And just like the old dens that we used to build from sofas, bits of furniture and rugs, we assembled our Northern Lights experience. First, the sheet over some furniture. Second, the fairy lights over the sheet. Third, a projection of our Northern Lights YouTube video. And, finally, some electronic chill-out tunes to relax us into our long wait, lying backwards and waiting for ... my friend to press 'play' on YouTube.

Much fun, laughter and dreaming were had that night. Would we ever see the Northern Lights? What was the easiest and cheapest way to see them? What else could we do if we were up there in twenty hours of darkness each day? The search engine started up.

And as if by magic, it happened: 'Northern Lights visible from north coast tonight.'

Now, to put this in perspective, we were on Ireland's south coast, in Cork, about six hours away by car from the north if we drove without stopping. It was also 7 p.m., about six hours away from when they were likely to start. And worse still, a couple of us had work the next day, and the rest had lectures. To top it all off, we weren't even guaranteed to see more than a glimmer in the sky.

Do we go? You bet!

Just like that, we were putting coats on and getting ready to go. One moment lying down in our Aurora Den, south of Cork, and the next, ready to do an all-nighter and drive hard. Spontaneity and adventure.

But just as we were heading out of the door, *someone* suggested something a bit too intelligent for my liking. There are lots of clouds outside right now. Should we check the cloud forecast for the north?

And so, the curtain came down on our adventure that night. Well, on that trip anyway. The rest of the evening was spent checking flight prices to Norway, Iceland and other spots, figuring out when it was best to go. Or was this something we wanted to keep for a special moment with that one person really close to us?

Regardless, it got us dreaming. And that was nearly as freeing as being there itself. Dreams that would go on and on and on, until they were fulfilled. Stories that would be told and told again about such hilarious nights dreaming!

## *Dreams fulfilled*

And so it was – we were now one step closer to dream fulfilment as we sat in the café in the Arctic Circle, retelling our Irish dreams that had got us to this point. Sadly, for us it was the wrong time of year. Unlike the Aurora during the winter, these nights in Norway would be filled with the 'greater light' that rules the day. A never-ending day. Twenty-four hours of pure daylight without ceasing. We were about to experience the Midnight Sun.

Just six months before I'd never even heard that such a thing existed. And now I was craving the experience.

My sister and I had always promised each other that we would do a marathon together. And as she was a missionary in sub-Saharan Africa, and I a university worker in Ireland, the opportunities were few and far between.

So, as a combination of many Christmas and birthday presents I'd never quite managed to get out to Africa for her, I decided this year would be our treat. A marathon that started at midnight, and there would still be blue skies and brightness, no matter what time we finished. Incredible! And to top it all off, a friend from university days, now an isolated Christian in the Arctic, was giving everything to us for virtually nothing.

Ever since that day, we've looked back, replayed the Norwegian music that we listened to on the road, pored over old photos and reminisced about the time I was running alongside the water and just fell in without anyone touching me, and we'd end up splitting our sides laughing.

## *Meet the Inventor of travel*

In a passage that even I managed to reach before I lost track of my New Year resolution to read through the Bible in a year, Genesis 1 and 2 tell us of the Inventor of travel.

'Be fruitful and increase in number; fill the earth and subdue it' (Genesis 1:28). There, implied in the very first commands to human beings: spread out over the earth – travel! You see, right from the start God makes an incredible world and gives us the freedom to roam and enjoy.[2] How good is that?

Just think a minute. What sort of world could God have made? Well, he could have made a black-and-white world. Perhaps one where human beings had such a long to-do list that they were just there to do stuff to keep him happy. Or maybe one where, after winding it up at the start, he could then be strangely like an absentee landlord, letting nature take its course as he watched with amusement, or as he busied himself with another universe.

But no, contrasted to the creation records of other religions and world views, the author of Genesis makes some very clear statements.

Here is a God who makes a rich diversity of a world. Pregnant with colour and brimming with life, it is both intricately designed and also stunningly majestic. It contains in it both the silence of the tranquil oasis pools in a hidden mountain valley and the roar of the ocean, relentlessly pounding the shores hour after hour. It holds not only the solid brown expanse of the sands of the endless Sahara Desert, but also the variety of green shrubbery and undergrowth that you'll find when you take a boat down the Mekong River in Laos. It boasts things that we have yet to fathom and discover at the most microscopic of levels, yet also the vast universes of planets, stars and space that even the finest of telescopes that humankind has ever made will struggle to comprehend. How amazing is that?

Here also is a God who claims to be distinct from the world, yet still very involved. Involved at the start, involved as he lives with his people and walks among them, and involved through his people as they follow his heart for the world.

And this world is not a product of the gods fighting one another for supremacy. It tells of the true Creator who makes things good, and makes humanity very good too.

## Think bigger! Two challenges to our perceptions

God saw all that he had made, and it was very good.
(Genesis 1:31)

### Finding good everywhere

*Traveller*: Dan Ross
*Means of travel*: Bike
*Time travelling*: One year
*Places travelled*: Everywhere between New Zealand and Ireland

*Nicest people*: 'It might surprise you, but they were in Iran. I didn't even have to spend a single night in paid accommodation. Everywhere I stopped people offered me the chance to join them for an incredible banquet of dates, rice dishes and tender kebab (like you've never seen before), or just to hang out, or anything I needed – it was incredible!'

Let's be honest, for many travellers, stories like Dan's make them unsure of the faith they were brought up with. If all these [insert religious people] are so nice, and yet so many of my Christian friends wouldn't be this kind, then does our faith, our personal relationship with Jesus, really make a difference in life? Baffled, several students I've known have thought of throwing in the towel with their faith, as they've moved from the supposedly narrow-minded monocultural setting of home and discovered the world to be a far richer, far more diverse experience than they ever could have imagined. The stereotypes of nations, peoples and religions are just frankly quite often nonsense.

There are several reasons why this may be the case. As I often host Couchsurfers (an online platform that allows travellers to exchange culture while staying on the sofas of local people), I've found my visitors are often overawed by the warmth and friendliness of the Irish people. But having experienced these, and having decided to come back and live in Ireland as a result, several have broken down in tears beside me as they've found this to be an entirely different proposition. It's all too easy to be nice to people you'll never see again, to whom you can show your favourite things, and for whom, even without language, the world can seem such an exciting place.

But beyond that reason, what we've seen from Genesis shows us that humans were created very good. And although the world has become broken and something seems to have gone wrong (more about that later), we've still got remnants of this 'very goodness' in us. And so, it shouldn't surprise us when some of the most religious cultures in this world are incredibly hospitable, even if they're not Christian. In fact, we should expect to find the most glorious flavours of 'very good' left in most people. Some have called it God's 'common grace'. That just means that he lavishes grace to everyone (regardless of belief), even if the world is now rebelling: '[God] sends rain on the righteous and the unrighteous' (Matthew 5:45).

Apart from expecting some remnant of 'very goodness', what else can we learn from such a creation account as we travel onwards?

## Goodness oozes from *all* things

*Traveller*: Sophie
*Means of travel*: On foot
*Time travelling*: Frequent weekend retreats
*Places travelled*: Anywhere off the beaten track

'I grew up loving any chance I had to escape the city. Hour after hour I spent watching the waves pounding the shore, hiking up hills to see views for miles around, or sitting in tranquil rest in the cleft of some rocks while the wind whistled by outside.

'Heading back to the rhythms of city life never seemed so romantic to me. I never understood people who could take city breaks – why go to a concrete urban jungle when you could go to a real rainforest instead? To me, God was far more present in the raw beauty of his supposedly untouched creation than he ever would be in tarmacked roads and skyscrapers, with people rushing frantically around doing their day's business.'

Sophie, like many of us, constantly equated serene experiences with spiritual ones, and struggled to relate God to the hustle and bustle of life. She had little room for seeing God present with us in city life.

But when we think like that, we are robbing ourselves of a God who is Lord over *every* area of creation and sees good in everything. Let's look at the great positive of cities too. They are larger hubs of humanity that can

- be great facilitators of art and creativity;
- lend themselves to institutions that specialize and offer expertise;
- develop beautiful things that help humanity;
- bring diverse people together, united by common goals.

People in smaller settlements would rarely experience or achieve all of the above. Cities have the potential to be exciting places where the great Architect God, whom we often associate just with stars, mountains, seashores and other majestic things, is still visible and reigning as we create buildings, spaces and so much more.

And it's travelling that often gets us thinking about these things, shaping our theology and making us come back to re-examine what we had always thought the Scriptures said. Really, it was often just our experiences speaking to us in the past.

We can still love retreats, immersing ourselves in nature and feeling the freedom of the outdoors, but hopefully now we can not only *stomach* city life, but seek to thrive under a God who has enabled cities to be enjoyed as much as the rest of his world, as he entrusts us to develop it in his image. Everything oozes his goodness, not just certain parts of creation.

## Think bigger with Dan and Sophie

Dan and Sophie's stories are slightly unusual, yet necessary, glimpses, to excite us about the type of God we follow. A God who commands travel in his second commandment to humanity is a travelling God. He shares our passions. Or better put, we share his. You see, our passions and desires, our dreaming and reminiscing, our thrill and our wonder are all instilled in us because of who our God is. If he hadn't made the world as he did, how could we ever dream about it? We're left trying to imagine what on earth God, being infinitely better and bigger than his creation, is like. Oomph! It sends my mind into a boggle and my heart a bit dizzy.

## Think bigger! A challenge to our pride

Having had our perceptions challenged by Dan and Sophie, there's one final challenge from what we have seen so far. Having a creation with humans playing such a central role could conceivably lend itself to arrogance on our part if we lose perspective. But as we read history we realize that we're just a few among the billions upon billions who have ever lived – one of many species, in just one of many galaxies. Any stopping to look at the stars, being caught up in storms on the oceans or beholding a tornado will soon remind us of that. We are tiny specks on an infinite platform. Here today, gone tomorrow.

And that's where most scientists finish: making ourselves feel small. That becomes the defining thing driving us towards an agnosticism that cries out for our brief years on this planet, 'We just don't know much.'

Popular scientist Brian Cox reminds us:

> Our picture of the universe is falling to bits. We've suddenly decided that 96% of the universe is made of something we've not yet discovered. Either that's wrong and there's something fundamental we don't know about our observations or it's right and we don't understand 96% of the universe.[3]

We know so little! Christians often read a Genesis narrative and see God's perspective, not *just* what we see with our eyes, discovering that humans are more than that. But we're quick to jump ahead in the story and not dwell on the fact that we are small and insignificant in the grand scheme of time!

But skipping this will give us problems in life, as we close the gap between an infinite and eternal God, and his finite and limited creation (us). Pride and an inflated image of ourselves will creep in very fast if we don't get the context. This might not seem like a problem until we find the circumstances of life overwhelming us and we've got nothing 'big' left to put them in perspective.

That 'bigness' of God is beautiful. Even my friends notice it and say to me, 'Peter, how can you always be productive and never seem to be consumed by any worries?'

## *In the land of the Midnight Sun*

And that's where all our travels can be powerful reminders of what we've seen so far: God's care for travel; God's incredible world made good in all parts; our place in creation. Travelling to see the Midnight Sun in Norway, where the temptation was to stay up all 'night' because it still appeared to be daylight, reminded me that I'm just human. I can't keep going through all those hours of daylight. Being lost in awe and wonder at such a phenomenon leaves me inspired by the Creator God, for whom even sunrises are simply a tiny flash of his greater power. One of the prophets in the Bible puts it this way:

> His splendour was like the sunrise;
>> rays flashed from his hand,
>> where his power was hidden.
> (Habakkuk 3:4)

I hope that travel leaves our hearts worshipping our great God to even deeper levels than before. But now we must go, as our lift has arrived to take us all the way down eastern Scandinavia till we find a train to take us onwards across the continent. The views should be stunning!

### Questions for the road

- What favourite aspects of creation show you who God is?
- How does the creation account free you to spot positive things in many world views and people, and not just in

Christians? How can you go about doing that in life, like Dan did?

- Did anything surprise you about what Sophie said? What do you think about cities pointing people to God?
- Do you ever lose perspective on the greatness of God? How can you let your travels restore this picture of who he really is?

---

### Prayer

Creator of the heavens and earth,
you are infinite and incredible.
Before anything was, you were.
We, as your creation, could spend all our lives exploring
this earth and still never exhaust your goodness to us in
the world you have given us.
And we know that you must be far more majestic and
beautiful than anything you have made.
Help us to see the world as you do,
to see all of it as yours, not just the sunsets and seas.
Help us to see all humans as you do, as people
in your image.
Teach us what it is to live before you,
in humility and reverence, all of our allotted days.
Warm our hearts with your beauty once again,
for Jesus your Son's sake,
Amen.

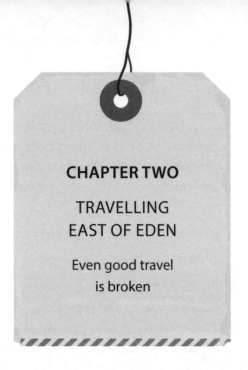

## CHAPTER TWO

### TRAVELLING EAST OF EDEN

Even good travel
is broken

We cannot go back. That's why it's hard to choose.
You have to make the right choice. As long as you
don't choose, everything remains possible.
(*Mr. Nobody*)[1]

***Destination***: China
***Weather***: Muggy, polluted air
***Company***: No-one for miles

Paralysis!

Somehow, I couldn't choose. How should I use my annual leave?

There were the friends getting married across the Irish Sea in England. It meant a weekend away, but because I always met lots of old university friends there, it was always a great laugh.

Then there was my sister whom I'd never visited in Africa. She is dear to my heart, and we get on so well. But her country isn't exactly a tourist resort. For my £1,000 round trip, I'd get to see her, use up most of my annual leave (of course, in order to make it worthwhile), become tired out from another culture, climate and language, and not have much more to show for it.

My housemates were all talking of a skiing trip that year too. It would be fantastic to get to know them better, and if I was the only one stopping the trip or missing out it would be awkward. But I'm not really a skiing fan, and the package did seem a bit luxurious.

And then there were the trips that would really help me know what to do with my life in the future. Friends, my church and I had always thought I'd got the right gifts for living among unreached people groups (i.e. those who'd never heard the gospel), so this was something obvious for me to do. What's more, missionary organizations were crying out for individuals to fill vacancies and meet needs. This would mean proactively exploring opportunities, matching skills and trying out lifestyles. But should it consume my annual holidays?

Lots of options and potential adventures, and that was without even considering that my work was already regularly taking me away from local church, friends and family: I wasn't often there for them without proper planning in advance. And I haven't even mentioned the bucket list that loomed large over my thought life, wooing my heart on a far more regular basis than the responsibilities of doing things like visiting my church's mission partners or relatives I hadn't seen for ages.

Because my thinking of potentially living abroad meant that all of my future was up in the air, I was in paralysis in other areas of my life too. What am I looking for if I go out with someone? Am I asking a girlfriend to be willing to go overseas with me, or to help me in ministry life here in Ireland?

Another paralysing decision.

Every week I'd feel that something would shift slightly in my calendar or in my list of things affecting my choices, and so I'd go back mentally and re-examine all the same stuff I examined the previous week to see whether anything was any clearer.

Evidently not.

## The nightmare of perpetual options

I was consumed. I knew that I could do any of the above for God's glory. I knew that all of them could become a fantastic part of him building his kingdom, and his Holy Spirit could use me, even if I picked horrible options.[2] God was good at that – turning anything into good, for those who were seeking to follow him. I mean, if he could use even the prophet Jonah who was running away from him, refusing to do what was being asked, or Joseph whose life seemed such a disaster following the jealousy and cruelty of his brothers, then he could use what I was trying to do for his glory! '[Joseph's brothers] intended to harm [him], but God intended it for good to accomplish what is now being done, the saving of many lives' (Genesis 50:20).

I knew I wasn't hunting the 'one path' of decisions that would make life perfect or easy, and that I should be free! But somehow it didn't feel like that at all. My desire for the best option still consumed me. Oh, how I longed to see everything clearly as black or white, bad or good. A murky grey seemed perpetually to loom over me like a cloud. Perhaps the holiday didn't matter as much as, say, my future, or my future wife (if God was going to lead me In that dIrectIon). All those choIces seemed all the more real, and scary consequences loomed over my shoulder.

The world was my oyster – but for the first time that didn't seem so nice. Perhaps I didn't like oysters after all. The unfettered freedom and choice that we spent all our lives chasing after had now crippled me into paralysis.

Wouldn't life just have been easier in my great-grandparents' generation, doing the job of my father, going to the school the family went to, travelling to the same holiday destination, and investing in the same circle of friends and relatives as they had invested in? Even the choice of spouse came from the local town rather than from the three billion or so of the opposite gender on this planet. How simple and beautiful!

Or would it be? For some brief moments of frustration every day I forget that I love options. Options are what I thrive on: to know that I could go off and switch career emphasis any time I want; to know I'm not missing out on anything because I have everything at my fingertips waiting for me. But far more important than the fear of missing out (FOMO, as some have called it) is to know that all possibilities are mine.

I want a god of options, because options make life comfortable for me. But, as one author put it, it's not the full story:

The god of open options is a cruel and vindictive god. He will break your heart. He will not let anyone get too close. But at the same time, because he is so spiteful, he will not let anyone get too far away because that would mean they are no longer an option. On and on it continues, exhausting and frustrating and confusing and endless, pulling towards and then pushing away, like the tide on a beach, never finally committing one way or the other. We have been like the starving man sitting in front of an all-you-can-eat buffet, dying simply because he would not choose between the chicken and the shrimp.

The god of open options is also a liar. He promises you that by keeping your options open, you can have everything and everyone. But in the end, you get nothing and no one.[3]

And that 'god of options' can be smartly dressed in a beautiful, Christian (modest) dress, with sparkly shoes. Options about how to invest one's life. Options of whom (or whether) to marry. Options of simply being so nuanced that in the end we never say anything of any importance.

But let's bring this back to our own lives as travellers. Sound familiar? It's the god that many of us encounter as soon as we dream up a bucket list, as soon as we have dilemmas of where to go, or whom to stay in touch with.

## Human or superhuman?

Extensive choices are the joys and real privileges of God's good gifts to us in this world. But it's our mismanagement of them and our failure to grasp our humanity and our createdness that gets us into trouble. Realistically, we can only go to a finite number of places, a finite number of times. We'll probably never visit everywhere we want to, nor find them in the picture-book state portrayed in the brochure if we do. We'll probably only be able to keep In touch with a certain number of close friends in any meaningful way, or else end up with many unfulfilling surface-level friendships.

We are humans. And instead of trying to kick against this fact, by seeking to be seen and to act at a superhuman level, we ought to delight in the reality of our humanity. Because our good Father made us to be this way for a reason, even before it all went sour with the rebellion that happened in Genesis chapter three, which we call the 'fall', leading to our 'broken' world. We were people who were made in a good world only to do so much. A day of rest was built into the fabric of creation for a reason: rest was good, right from the start.

> By the seventh day God had finished the work he had been doing; so on the seventh day he rested from all his work. Then God blessed the seventh day and made it holy, because on it he rested from all the work of creating that he had done.
> (Genesis 2:2–3)

I learned this the hard way in my first few years of work. Travelling around the large region where I worked, I was often away from home three nights a week, sleeping on friends' sofas, staying up late chatting to them, getting up early and filling my free time with lots of things, from long-distance running to playing field hockey, to staying out late socializing with friends, and much more. Life was full, and I loved it.

In fact, I would sometimes deliberately put too much in my diary for the day, knowing that because we live in a world that is broken, something would probably not happen. A student may not show up for a Bible study. A summer volunteer team may be cancelled. A friend won't mind if a meeting I'd scheduled too close to another overruns and I'm late. How's that for understanding a broken world and making it work in my favour? (Please don't try this at home!)

But sadly, as I ran around at a hundred miles an hour, something had to give.

I walked into my doctor's practice one morning, having felt all over the place for a few days before. Unbeknown to me, the letter he gave me for Accident and Emergency sent me straight to the front of the queue, on to a trolley and with porters sprinting straight for intensive care, while no-one else around me knew what was happening.

I had been diagnosed with some form of diabetes and was on the dangerous point of passing out if they didn't act fast.

To this day, the doctors will tell me that it wasn't related to anything in my life that I could have acted upon. But regardless, it made me slow down, stop and think about my life, and about why I struggled so much with having diabetes and needing to inject myself every day.

With modern-day treatments, the physical hassle of injections and taking blood-sugar tests regularly was not difficult, or even anything that involved any mental energy. It became routine. And yet I still struggled.

What was hurt far more that day in hospital was the blow to my pride. Up to that moment the world was my oyster, and I could run on and on and pretend I was superhuman, saving different situations, excelling at work and those things I put my hand to in my free time.

But that day made me realize there was a doctrine that I said I believed in that was still far from my joy. I was a human. And a broken human at that.

It sounds so stupid, so silly, that *anyone* would deny this. But all over the world, people of every world view, tribe and religion (or lack thereof) are trying to deny this very thing every time they try and take control of some part of life by themselves.

> Unless the Lord builds the house,
>     the builders labour in vain.
> Unless the Lord watches over the city,
>     the guards stand watch in vain.
> In vain you rise early
>     and stay up late,
> toiling for food to eat –
>     for he grants sleep to those he loves.
> (Psalm 127:1–2)

The daily reminder of my frailty and (broken) humanity from my diabetes meant that for the first time in my life I started to try to delight in being a human. Physically, as I said, it didn't make a huge difference to me, although perhaps it made me slightly less capable of endless nights with little sleep, and running marathons became a slightly more difficult mental exercise in balancing sugar levels. But mentally and spiritually, it freed me never to think of myself any more than I ought. I am a human. And just one among billions. Jesus has saved the world, and I don't need to. And if I don't get round to all of my options in life? Well, that's OK. God can raise up others to do things I can't, or allow me to enjoy even better options in the new heaven and the new earth that are to come!

Suddenly, I was even freed up to enjoy things I thought were mundane. Sleep had always been just a necessity, and a rather boring one at that: sleeping hours were wasted hours when I wasn't doing anything fun or productive. I was not sleeping for God's glory. But now, sleeping hours expressed my humanity and trust in God! If he woke me up to a new day, he was being merciful.

Put in perspective, there is much that humanity has been created to be that can legitimately be celebrated. But when it gets out of control, and we desire to be more than that, as a result of the fall, our world will turn chaotic.

And that's what the Bible describes in the early chapters of Genesis as 'travelling east'.

## *Photos of an ancient problem*

I am always telling students that when we read the Bible, it's not the random thought that strikes us that we should primarily take away (much as God sometimes does use random thoughts), but the main point that God (through the author) wants to convey. And often how we find out the main point is through digging deeply into the text, depending upon God's Holy Spirit to open our eyes to the intimacy of his words as they act in our lives. When repeated phrases come up, alarm bells should start ringing, and we should take note.

So it is in Genesis 3 – 14 with the word 'east' (3:24; 4:16; 11:2; 12:8; 13:11). It's not a major riff, but still it's repeated often, and in particular seems to be something that symbolizes a people moving away from God's land – the place of his presence. Let's use our cameras and take a few snapshots of that journey east, into places where humans thought more of themselves than they ought to have done, and suffered paralysis as a result.

## Snapshot 1

In Genesis 3 we have our first example of humans wanting to be more than human, as Adam and Eve eat of the tree of the knowledge of good and evil and desire to be as God. It appears that they exit the paradise of the Garden of Eden to the east, or at least that's where the angels are guarding. This banishment is an act of judgment, for sure, but also an act of grace, as no-one would want a place of God's holy presence to be spoilt by sin. And so, long term, this is a gracious act, to remove the horrors of evil from a paradise. But in the meantime, they're left wandering without a home.

## Snapshot 2

In Genesis 4, after a similarly horrific act of human independence, pretending to be the one who has authority to take life, Cain is forced to pack his bags and head east, to be known as a wanderer, paralysed by not knowing where he is going or to what name he belongs. It's judgment again, but it's also grace, as Cain is allowed to live, even after the terrible act of murdering his brother.[4]

## Snapshot 3

In Genesis 11 we see the people moving eastwards still, which gives us a flavour that what is to come in the story will not be wonderful news. More judgment, because the people want to 'de-God God'[5] by making a name for themselves. Ironically, whoever they are, their names aren't recorded, and instead we get the list of names ('the account of Shem' in Hebrew means 'a name') of a bunch of nobodies through whom God graciously builds his lineage.

Unsurprisingly, as before, where humans want to make a name for themselves, paralysis on the building site ensues, as linguistic barriers make for an infuriating setting. And I wonder whether God's scattering of the people across the earth after Babel is another gracious act, as they're no longer said to be moving east all the time.

Instead, it's the start of God setting the scene for the promises he's about to make to Abram (in Genesis 12), that he'll bless all nations and all peoples through him. Abram is recorded as not having gone as far east as Ai, and stopping (in verse 8) to build an altar and call 'on the name of the LORD' – quite a contrast to those who wanted to build themselves a name.

## A final snapshot

The only other eastern mention in these chapters is sadly that of Lot, who chose foolishly to live in the east, which selfishly seemed like the far better location to the human eye, but he suffered the consequences. Yet, still God persisted in lavishing grace upon Lot, sending a rescuer in Abram to save his family from destruction.

These riffs of judgment, moving east into paralysis (away from God's land, and his presence and perfect rule), and yet with grace intertwined, bring five things to mind for us travellers of how this rubric of seeing the world affects us.[6]

## Lessons from the reality of a broken world

### 1. Suffering communication paralysis

After five days into cycling through China, Dan was incredibly lonely. There was only so much skyping home you could do without spending a fortune. But apart from that, there was no-one to talk to. I mean, he could try. But it was futile. International sign language (the unofficial variety) would get him the food he needed, and sometimes, if he was fortunate enough, a bed for the night. But with no Chinese apart from what he could search for online, he was alone. Alone in one of the most populated countries on earth.

As I write this, I am sitting in the hills behind Nice in France at a work conference. I'm excited to return to a Francophone land, because I studied French all through school and have tried to keep it up ever since. Although our conference (only ten delegates) is in English, some of the participants struggle with English, so we frequently burst into French and have some translated sessions too.

But sadly, my ability to respond quickly to anything that is said has gone down the drain! Understand? Yes, completely! But respond well? Not a chance! The frustrations of sitting here unable to communicate or take part in the hilarious banter sends me back to infantile status.

What is equally annoying is that even my English isn't connecting. Humour that on any other day in Ireland would stir a room is falling on deaf ears and even getting antagonistic looks from my American friends. Even in my own language I am failing to communicate!

And there's something both beautiful and utterly frustrating about that. When I try and make a name for myself (in small ways) by holding a room with a story or a joke, I'm quickly reminded that cross-cultural communication frustrates that. What happened in the 'east' at Babel still has long-lasting effects, even in a world that tries to unite again around a common international language (English).

## 2. When our story dominates

The often-subconscious temptation of travellers to 'out-story' each other quickly comes to an end, not necessarily through language limitations but simply through humanity's unwillingness constantly to hear of travels, however insightful and interesting, because of the one-directional nature of the communication. The supposedly enlightened traveller tells those of us who are not as privileged to have jobs, finance or lack of family responsibility, about their extensive travels, their wonderful learning.

Haven't we all been there? And we must be careful that this highly self-centred preoccupation doesn't come with a thin veneer of Christian coating of doing 'mission'.

Instead, finding our place in the bigger (God's) story, we find true stories that have been told and retold thousands of times over, in various cultures, at points throughout all history, and yet have never grown old. This big story of God's grace, bringing a travelling people home to a vibrant new world to explore and enjoy, is far better news when told well than any travel story ever could be.

### 3. Misjudging fellow travellers

As travellers we are not only often guilty of being consumed with our own travels, or in small ways our own name, but also often victims of those who needlessly judge, and do so far too quickly.

The comparison game is a human favourite. Like that old childhood game called 'Top Trumps' where children have a themed collection of cards to compare and swap. Speaking personally, as a family of ornithologists, for us it was birds. If I called out 'the largest wingspan', then if anyone could beat the statistic on my card, they would get my card and would then call a category on the card. Constantly comparing in order to achieve superiority and victory was the objective.

If your heart is anything like mine, we can be very quick to compare ourselves with others. If we see someone else travelling more than us, we can question their motives or tend towards jealousy. Simply posting pictures on social media can generate storms of reactions from Christians: 'He is always posting up holiday pictures – has he no idea of sacrifice?'

But like most things in life, we'd do well to avoid such quick judgments here. What if someone's work enables him to do these travels? What good purpose or motive is in his heart as he posts these pictures – could it be one of wanting others to enjoy

God's world? Could he actually be spending less money than us, even though he's travelling the world?

All these are quite possible scenarios, and in a changing world travel isn't necessarily a sign of privilege any more. My housemate who travelled the world for a year found that he spent less than I did at home and living quite conservatively in Ireland!

So, let's think twice before expressing judgment.

## 4. When travelling is tough

Although travel, and in particular pleasure travel to other countries, may not solely be for those from privileged back-grounds like it used to be, it is still true that for many it remains a distant dream. Two things remind us of this.

The first is the images that strike our news screens of thousands of Syrian refugees piling on to tiny inflatables in vast numbers in pursuit of their paradise trip to Europe, and away from the nightmare of a war-torn existence and the ravages of simply trying to exist.

The second lies closer to home (in every sense of the term) for me, and it is the awareness of those around us who, for health reasons or otherwise, cannot travel. Although the world is slowly getting more accessible, there are many among us who suffer greatly, who can only dream of participating in a simple holiday.

A close relative of mine has suffered from a fairly unknown, long-term autoimmune disease that has sometimes left her without the ability to walk far, often without sleep and frequently in pain. The doctors seem to celebrate even when they can just put a name on the condition. A cure has so far been beyond them. The outdoor life she used to enjoy up mountains and watching birds while clambering over rocks, has largely turned into staying in one place, sometimes being driven to locations where she can see birds through binoculars.

The pictures on social media could be both a joy and a pain, possibly at once. Joy at seeing the world God has made. But pain at no longer being able to be the photographer and see with the lenses that God has given her.

I'm sure there are people in your life like this, or maybe worse off, even in our privileged cultures, not to mention the rest of the world. By thinking of these people before we plan for or depart on our travels, we can help make travel a blessing to many more people than just ourselves. Perhaps it'll mean going somewhere they can go, doing something for them while we're away, or staying around home and going for day trips instead. Yet, for the sake of the poorest in our world, we'll have to think even further – how can we give sustainably to help poverty-stricken people in a way that will empower them? (Sadly, the question is too complex to do justice to in a short book, but turn to the endnotes to help you start thinking through this topic.[7])

### 5. 'I love you, but . . . would you mind giving me some space?'

It is not just those who cannot travel whom the effects of a broken world lie heavy upon. Even among our own group of carefully hand-picked travellers we will find the effects of the fall displayed in this world. How do you decide whom to travel with? In my case, I soon found out that even the friends I got on best with, and had lived with, could still be a bit too much 24/7.

With varying priorities of how to spend money and time, with different interests and hobbies, a multiplicity of ways of relating to each other and so many methods of relaxing, we can infuriate even those we love dearly. Often, travel intensifies the experience of having to bear with each other patiently. Times of explosive anger, or the 'silent treatment', doled out when things get too much, or simply the individualism that constantly makes us think of ourselves and our own interests, will not be far away from those who spend all day, every day with each other.

## Beautiful ruins

These are just a few of the areas of this world and our humanity that we see tarnished since humanity started rebelling against what we were made to be. The apostle Paul describes it like this: 'We know that the whole creation has been groaning as in the pains of childbirth right up to the present time' (Romans 8:22). Blaise Pascal painted the same thing slightly differently when he said: 'Man is the glory and the shame of the universe.'[8] But although every area of the world's make-up has been ruined by sin, this does not mean that it is as bad as it possibly can be in every area.

I love finding hidden travel spots where no-one else has been. The danger is that in sharing them on my Instagram feed, and getting thirty extra 'likes' (it was worth it, right?), and everyone else doing the same, word gets out, and soon a major travel blog has featured the place, and no-one can any longer enjoy the peaceful serenity that once was! In the same way, travel guidebooks are seen as both a real blessing and an absolute curse to places.

If the rumour of terrorism (even if no great threat) didn't go against the possibility of a tide of tourists swarming to these unseen places, I might not have posted them in the first place. But from the words of my hire car company behind the desk, I figured my photos probably wouldn't be in any danger of igniting a tourist tsunami in the region.

'You want to hire a car? Where will you go? What do you mean you don't have a group with you? Where is your hotel, your tour guide and your package?'

It was obvious that the rep had never seen two lads in their twenties go off unaccompanied and explore his beautiful country before. But shocked as he was, he let us hire and we arrived at some of the most stunning Roman ruins in the world – this, coming from an Irishman who has castle ruins in every field for miles around.

Despite them being broken and dilapidated ruins, there was something utterly stunning about them. Something majestic remained even several thousand years on.

Beautiful ruins.

And that's how the reality is that we're left with after the fall. Lots of good still a remnant from creation, yet bitterly broken and ruined good

## *Travelling onwards*

So, what should that cause us to expect as we travel? That fine line between 'beautiful' and 'ruin' is a hard one to see and grasp in the world. We all love to go to one extreme or the other and declare something to be either completely good or totally evil. But the messy reality of this world is that there is more grey than we'd like to think. Even in the most evil individuals in history there were some very good human desires and traits. Even in the most incredible of Christians, or any human, there is the potential to lose it and display a very dark streak or character trait within.

But although it is far harder to live and travel in a world like this, it is a factor that makes me believe that the Christian world view is true. The Russian Alexander Solzhenitsyn describes it like this:

> If only it were all so simple! If only there were evil people somewhere insidiously committing evil deeds, and it were necessary only to separate them from the rest of us and destroy them. But the line dividing good and evil cuts through the heart of every human being. And who is willing to destroy a piece of his own heart?[9]

No other world view leaves such a balance of beautiful ruin. Many other religions will tell us of a world essentially good at heart. Secular humanism tends towards painting a story of selfish genes, ruthlessly evolving with no reason to expect pro-longed good, or no way to define the same.

Is there any way to describe this world's beautiful ruin of a condition?

And that is why I'm guessing people veer between describing travel as incredibly good and throwing it away as rubbish only to be brought out in an emergency. Because so very few of us can live well with tensions in life – they can be exhausting.

Yet, that's what we're all set to do as we head out on the road one more time. This time we've got camels to take us where we need to go – to the Middle East and beyond. But like everything else in this chapter, one day of riding a camel and you'll discover they're not all the fun they're made out to be. You'll be a very broken traveller at the end of this day. Don't say I didn't warn you!

## Questions for the road

- Are there any ways in which you fail to see your humanity and try to live a superhuman life, or at least appear that way to others?
- Which do you struggle with more: seeing the beauty left in humanity or seeing the ruin of it all?
- Who, or what, in life do we have a tendency either to hold up as completely good or think of as utterly wrong?
- Which of the five ways of experiencing a broken world has most impacted on you? Are there other things that have shown you the brokenness of the world as you have travelled?

### Prayer

Lord Jesus,
we come and we confess to you that we are
imperfect travellers.
Forgive us when we try to live as more than created
humans, here today and gone tomorrow.
Forgive us when we are so paralysed by the good
things in this world that we struggle to live.
Forgive us when we get consumed by the negative
things outside ourselves in creation, in where we travel,
in those whom we travel with and in those we've
left behind at home.
Help us instead to see the very real problems in our
own hearts first.
And for every time we realize them, would you help
us a hundred times over to see Jesus,
who, being in very nature God, did not consider equality
with God something to be grasped, but took on the
nature of a servant, being made in human likeness,
and through death on a cross came to restore the
beautiful ruin to a state beyond any beauty we have ever
yet seen or known, but have glimpsed in him alone.
Teach us what your grace and judgment
look like as we live.
And make us more like yourself as we travel.
Amen.

## CHAPTER THREE

## TRAVELLING THE WORLD WITH NEW LENSES

Seeing God's panorama
of travel

There are no foreign lands.
It is the traveller only who is foreign.
(Robert Louis Stevenson)[1]

**Destination**: The Middle East
**Weather**: Oppressive heat
**Company**: Tourist

'I'm never going back again.'
'I wouldn't go there for more than two days.'
'They were so aggressive.'
'I felt so overwhelmed all the time and unable to escape.'

Comments you wouldn't expect to find in a holiday brochure for Egypt. Nonetheless, it was the expressed sentiment as soon as the air hostesses had shut the aeroplane door on the flight to

Manchester, and the tourist might as well have been back on home turf again.

And yet, these weren't angry comments. Not at all. More just baffled. Because the next sentence would always reaffirm that they did really enjoy their trip. But did they? Was this masochistic enjoyment?

It's 45 degrees Celsius and you've headed out for the day in Cairo. Dressed in as little as possible for a relatively conservative country like Egypt, you have a phone in one pocket for photos and your wallet in the other. Apart from a few sights, the main 'attraction' for most people is spending the day walking around quaint *souk* (market) stalls in tiny alleyways.

It's a maze of tiny stalls, each repeating very similar wares, yet every one unique and with its own quirky personality that probably reflects the owner as he stands there. A true joy to browse.

'Sir, sir! Come here! Look, no buy.'

At which you are greatly pleased. Aha! I can look at all these things and not be forced to buy. Perfect. And so, you walk in.

A few minutes of polite chit-chat with the stallholder later and you start to browse. Taking an interest in a couple of things in particular, you discuss one and take a photo. And the stall-owner moves in for the kill, with you their unsuspecting prey.

'You like?'
'Erm . . . yes, it's beautiful' (not meaning to offend).
'Well, I give you good price.'
'How much is it?'
'A good price. What would be a good price for you?'
'Oh well, I don't know.'
'Well, I'll offer you a special Ramadan price of 240 (Egyptian) pounds. Normally I would sell it for 410 pounds, but my brother specially made this one, and so I am able to get it for you far cheaper for you alone today.'

Wow, you think. Such a good offer just for me. And his brother made it . . . so it's really authentic. But eleven euros . . . just for that? Oh, but it's genuine, and when else could you buy something like this? And so, the internal debate rages on.

'Oh, I think I'll think about it and come back to you later.'

Sensing his prey moving onwards, the stall-owner puts himself between you and the door and tries again.

'Oh, my friend, this is a one-time offer. My brother only made one. Look at how bad the quality of the normal "tourist" ones is! This is a special one for you. You are English. Cheaper prices than Asda for you.'

At which you'd still love to walk out of the shop, but you start to wonder whether he is, in fact, absolutely correct. It does indeed appear better than the others. And it would be fun to have.

And so, as you pull out your wallet, you hesitantly try another ten pounds off the price. At which you feel stupid, as this poor man quickly says he couldn't afford to sell them for that price, and reverts back to the original. And the deal is done. The robbery has happened.

The only consolation: you probably could afford to be robbed for the joy of such an exchange. A masochistic joy. Paying perhaps more to experience the culture than for the item itself, you now walk out to try and squeeze it into your hand luggage. It will soon sit in some cupboard, not in use, back home.

And unless you understand the culture, this repetition all day will break you.

Anger.

Frustration.

How could they?!

You walk into another stall, determined for the same thing not to happen again.

'Hello sir! Look, no buy!'
'*No*! Just tell me how much it is!'
'What would be good price for you, sir?'

The man looks so honest. And somehow, I spurt out a figure. And in a split second of madness I wonder whether I'm dealing with a reincarnated man from the last stall. And my Egyptian pounds, which once were a good exchange rate against the Euro, have just somehow vanished in euro-like quantities.

But why does this happen? Why can't they just deal normally with me? Why do I always feel so guilty about walking away once I've started talking to them?

And therein lies the problem.

## *Life back home*

You see, we all come from a culture. And none of us can ever shake that culture off. No matter how much travel we do, how many countries we live in, and however smug we may feel compared with those (supposedly) backward people who are still living at home with their parents, we're still enculturated. Because cultures operate on various value systems that mean that although you can understand each culture, and perhaps analyse it very effectively, it is still impossible to step outside all culture completely, because you'll still fall somewhere on that value-system scale.

Let's make it real. Go back to my unfortunate passengers on the aeroplane, coming home from their Middle Eastern holiday. What went wrong?

In Britain it is likely they were brought up in what is sometimes called a guilt–innocence culture.[2] This means various things, but here are a few examples that might resonate with you. If you were to steal, but get away with it, most likely you would still feel guilty, and it would play on your mind (because it is wrong, you would say). If you were to turn up late to a wedding, it is likely the wedding would have started without you, unless you are the bride or some other significant part of the ceremony, of course (because your lateness is a fault on your part – you failed at the task of getting there on time). If you get asked for feedback on something a friend has done for you, you are most probably going to be quite direct in what you think can be improved, perhaps after saying a few positive things first (because you would desire to be truthful, even if it was hard for the listener to hear).

All of these things are products of a culture that loves to think of things in terms of right and wrong, guilt and innocence.

### *Holiday explained*

The tourists approaching the market stall wanted to tell the truth and were concerned about the task at hand – could they get what they wanted for a cheap price? The thing is, they assumed the market stallholder also had the same values. But as was very evident, he was most concerned not only for the price he was getting but also for being perceived to be an honourable man. He would not only negotiate a fair price, but would tell stories of authenticity, and would delight to get to know the customer as a human being (even sitting down to chat over mint tea, quite often), not just as a potential target for a sale.

Our market stallholder came from a shame–honour setting. The biggest goal for him was his honour. This does not mean he cared nothing for truth, but, stereotypically, the following could perhaps be said to be true examples of this culture.

If you got stopped by a police officer for breaking the speed limit, you would possibly chat for a long time, ask about the officer's family, find connections in society, and then pay a small bribe to be let free (because bribes are just the assumed way of paying for things for those on low salaries, and the employer depends on them as top-ups). If you went ahead with a business meeting without another person who was meant to be there being present, It would be a shameful thing – people matter! And you probably wouldn't be asked for any direct feedback, but instead would show someone did a good job by honouring them in other ways, especially public ones.

And so, in our holiday scenario, you can see why it's hard! Most of us who come from guilt–innocence scenarios can see no way to 'win' apart from being robbed of our money. We must tell the truth. We must be direct. We must accomplish the task at hand.

### Lenses and cultures

All this wouldn't be a huge problem (apart from the frustration on holiday) until we realize that we all read our Bibles and other cultures through our own cultural 'lenses' (or 'way of seeing things'). And in fact, this problem doesn't stop there, for even atheists and those holding to other world views will often claim that we're just seeing things from our limited perspective. When we first encounter that argument put persuasively by someone, or through experiencing another world view, it can be a powerful challenge to us in our faith.

We interpret every Bible story written down through our own lenses. Have you ever wondered why Jesus made such a big deal over Simon the Pharisee not washing his feet, drying them and putting perfume on them (Luke 7)? In our culture this is not really a big deal. And physically speaking, nor was it in theirs either. OK, your feet would be a bit yucky, but why was that a major problem to kick up a fuss about? In shame–honour culture it was far more of a thing. Not to do this to your guest was to shame them. And to be outdone by a disreputable prostitute-type figure, the one who did perfume Jesus' feet, was even more shameful.

Similarly, many of us who come from more task-orientated backgrounds would agree with Judas and any Pharisees when they moan at the amount of money wasted on perfuming Jesus' feet (John 12:4–5). It could be used for mission trips! But instead, Jesus welcomes such honour-inducing behaviour, flowing from a heart of worship and the realization of who he is. Because honour is important. And the perfume signified the purpose for which Jesus came – the death that was to follow – a point that the objection seemed to miss completely.

The significance of the passage is massively reduced if we read it purely through our guilt–innocence lenses. And so it is, as we look at other cultures and see their perspective on time, money, communication and hospitality. Issues that play central roles in some cultures are seen as side issues or luxuries by others. Quite often we'll assume our superiority and look on and see other cultures as sinful.

### Good news in our culture

As if how we view one another isn't messy, it also changes the shape of the good news we proclaim. You see, someone from a guilt–innocence culture might summarize the good news like this:

- God created us very good.
- After the fall we are each guilty before God.
- Jesus lived an innocent life, free from sin.
- Jesus died on our behalf, taking our guilt and punishment.
- Jesus rose again to defeat sin and death.
- Anyone who trusts in him will go to be with him for ever
  in a perfect place.

But the trouble is that although this is arguably a narrative that is a fair (but not complete) way of summarizing some gospel truth, it has very little to say to the person from a shame–honour background. Why have our gospel methods and summaries not made big inroads into communities like many Islamic ones, or even my own Irish one? Well, partly it's because we're speaking a different language!

## *Good news in the right language*

So, what should our gospel summaries be saying? Now, I don't wish to demean gospel summaries. I learned many as a kid, still use them, and think they've been a huge help to my spirituality, even as I remind myself of the good news each day. But I tend to find that those from shame–honour backgrounds don't much value logical systems of propositional truth, packaged in neat Western logic, for the task of sharing quickly with an individual.

But if they did, I could imagine they would echo those huge swathes of Scripture that speak into the shamefulness of sin, which exerts itself right from hiding in the Garden of Eden through to the eternal exposure of being constantly found out in the presence of God's judgment after death. It would speak of the death of Christ, who, 'for the joy that was set before him . . . endured the cross, scorning its shame' (Hebrews 12:2), so that 'the one who trusts in him will never be put to shame' (1 Peter 2:6).

## The Bible speaks into all cultures

What was once thought to be a Western–Eastern divide, in terms of cultures that had shame–honour lenses and others that had guilt–innocence ones, is now seemingly known to be far more nuanced. Many in the area where I grew up tried to convince me that guilt–innocence culture was inherently biblical, and that the West thinks like that because of our Judeo-Christian heritage. But the tricky thing is that, as we've briefly seen, when we read the Bible, it speaks of both guilt and shame. Both innocence and honour. And some Western cultures (like Ireland) are perceivably far more shame–honour.[3]

The implications of this are huge for those interested in God's Church being built across the nations. For example, Christian Union (mission team) events weeks in universities are generally high-profile, with thousands getting a chance to hear and respond to the gospel of Jesus in a relatively short space of time. In addition to the normal committee that runs the all-year-round mission team on campus, we form a new committee for the week of events.

It was our first evening meeting as a committee. I'd cooked them food so that they could get to know one another first, before any decisions needed to be made. But towards the end of the meal I very cheekily (knowing that such directness was not usually culturally appropriate) asked for their names (fine), courses (fine), years (fine), and why they wanted to be on the committee (not so appropriate). As all the Irish students one by one gave their reasons for being part of the week, their responses could be summed up by these two phrases:

'I wanted to feel more a part of things here in the community.'
'Ah sure, it'll be good craic.'

Visibly disturbed by such lack of passion for God, the one student from a more British culture on the committee blurted out: 'I love God and want to make him known to everyone. I think we should all be passionate for mission and want to grow in our understanding and practice of it.'

When I spoke to him later, he grabbed me and, looking rather panicked, asked: 'Peter, why does no-one care about mission on this, erm, mission committee?'

But these largely hand-selected students on the mission committee weren't apathetic about mission. What had happened was that I'd just asked a question that had the potential for some to feel shame in a new group. What if these young believers were exposed to not expressing themselves well in theologically nuanced statements about why they were there? And wasn't the whole purpose to build the honour of the group by saying that it would be a pleasure to work together on these things and get to know each other more?

And so they answered in a very relational way, to build honour.

Now, we've just had the chance to delve into one cultural issue, but there are hundreds of them that shape life, although not many that loom as large as the one above, which, naturally, has many cultural and theological implications flowing from it.[4]

## What does this mean for us travellers?

There used to be a British TV character who'd walk around constantly yelling out, 'Don't panic, don't panic!', but his cries often betrayed the very panic that was so evident in himself. And I think it's good advice for us here too. We could easily feel overwhelmed trying to get our heads around other cultures, and wonder whether we've missed the whole point of Scripture when doing so, but I think we can delight in one main thing: a faithful reading of the Bible together will get us to the right place.

God is faithful to his word and has chosen to reveal himself by it. The things that we need to know clearly are very clear. And the things we don't need to be so adamant about are not so clear. We can be confident that none of this cultural analysis will suddenly make us discover a new gospel thousands of years later that no-one managed to get right before!

### God gives us certainty

It appears quite obvious to me that Luke and John, as they record their eyewitness accounts of the Lord Jesus, seem to think that we can be certain about what we believe about Jesus, God's Son, and about salvation. Luke writes, 'so that you may know *the certainty* of the things you have been taught' (Luke 1:1–4), and John similarly, 'so that you may *know* that you have eternal life' (1 John 5:13–14).

Fellow travellers, don't let our doubts from our travels, and seeing other cultures and ways of life, rob us of that core certainty. Why not use them instead as a springboard to talk with others whom you trust, and see your confidence in Christ restored and grow even more in your awareness of his beauty amid the diversity of world views and ways of living?

**God helps us to understand his word**

But this confidence doesn't give us any excuses for laziness. Instead, it makes us careful as we handle the historical texts of Scripture. As has been said so many times before, the Scriptures were first of all written in the context of the time, to a particular audience, long before they were written to us (see the diagram here).

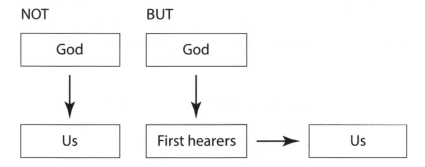

And to confirm that this is a principle from the Bible, we only have to look at passages such as Hebrews 3:7 where we'll notice the writer saying to his readers, 'As the Holy Spirit says', but then quoting a psalm written several hundred years before! What God has said, he still says today.

(There are plenty of other resources that more extensively expand on this,[5] so I won't say more here.)

## *What good does travelling do?*

Technically as we've seen before, we should be able to figure out what the Bible says without ever travelling. But, in reality, much of Scripture comes alive to us as we pass through various experiences of life, and thus much of it came alive to me as I travelled. Being away from the daily rhythms of life can leave us exposed and in a learning posture, in a way that staying with the familiar at home does not.

Visiting the Middle East and working alongside Arabs, I began to understand why certain stories were far more powerful than I'd ever realized. Walking the arid gorges and roads, with outcrops of rock that cast dark shadows over parts of my way, I understood why the priest, the Levite and others passed the man beaten up on the road from Jericho to Jerusalem, before the good Samaritan came to the rescue. It was scary indeed when the sun started to set.

Seeing sheep and goats in the wilds of an African desert enabled me to see why there could be some difficultly separating sheep from goats at the end times (Matthew 25:31–46), which seems implicit in the passage when some are surprised that they're not going to be with Jesus for ever, though they thought they'd played a good game.

I didn't learn any new truth as I travelled that I hadn't already heard in years of Bible teaching in faithful churches, but my experience of that truth did deepen as I learned more about what it was like for the original hearers, and therefore what I can rely on today to be the application too.

And that will always be the same each time I come back to Scripture. I am unlikely to find anything startlingly new in doctrine, but I am hoping that the Holy Spirit will deepen my understanding of old truths and lead me to see the implications of those for my life, the Church and the world.

We are clearly shown in Scripture that the experience that will most change us will not necessarily be the travel experience, but that of sitting in church hearing the preaching of God's word week by week, as our teaching elders rightly connect it to God's world by the power of God's Holy Spirit. If this is being done well, both in terms of handling God's word and speaking into culture in God's world, then no amount of travel will ever be able to replace faithful attendance at church week by week. All you ever need for godliness will be there, all you ever need to be like Jesus. And all experienced from frail, human lips. Baffling! But oh, so wonderfully good!

And it's good for people like my friend Seamus too.

**Traveller**: Seamus O'Sullivan
**Means of travel**: Bus pass
**Time travelling**: Rarely
**Places travelled**: A 20-mile radius of home

'I've a condition that I was born with that means I can't walk very far. It's really annoying when I see everyone else in the world travelling, but I've never been to any of these places.

'What I do instead is help out every week at the local international student café, which reaches out to people from around the world with the good news of Jesus. It's fantastic there – we've met people from fifty-six different countries in this last year alone – some from places you'd never dream of going to!

'We may struggle to have the same intensity of experience as we would have travelling first-hand to those places, but nonetheless I learn so much about how other cultures read the Bible and how they see the world that I'm convinced that pleasure travel is not necessary just to find out these things. Some day I'll get a passport and travel, but for now I'm praying God will give me contentment as I serve him here with the nations on our doorstep.'

Even though I know this to be true, and like Seamus I pray for contentment too, there are some things that still make my heart flutter as I see God at work.

### Divine appointments

One night I was driving the two hours from Waterford to Limerick (Ireland) around dusk. I was in a rotten mood, and far from making the most of my regular long car journey for work. Bitter about the day's events, and still replaying the conversations I'd had over and over again in my head, I pulled over to a hitchhiker on the roadside by a farm in a rural village. The public bus service in these parts was at best poor, and it was getting on for nightfall. The hitcher was a man of about my age, with flowing ginger beard and a waft of stereotypically Irish ginger hair.

His first question was to determine where I was going, followed shortly by his second: 'What is a Christian?'

Slightly stunned by such a question, given there was nothing in my car to suggest I would know, and bearing in mind that everyone in Ireland reckons they're Christians so don't ask, I stumbled to ask him why he was asking.

'You've a Northern accent. You must know. I mean Protestant and Catholic and all that. Y'know?'

But as I was sure he'd met many a Northerner before, I persisted. 'But what raises the question?'

It turned out he'd been travelling round the world for a year and had ended up in Hawaii. So beautiful was the experience with the community he'd met there that he decided to stay on and get to know them. Time was running out, but he wanted what they had that made them so joyful and servant-hearted. So, they said to him, 'Look, we run this summer volunteer programme in Haiti – you should go and find us there. Go home and raise funds, and we'll see you out there!'

And he had done so. His family thought he'd met a cult. 'I know they said they were Christians, but that can mean anything from those "born-agains" to cults,' they warned. 'Stay clear of it.' But it got him thinking, 'What is a Christian?' And so he asked the next person he met, who happened to be me driving along. Four minutes later we'd reached his brother's house, and he jumped out. All that we'd established was that the group was Youth With A Mission, that he should trust them and go, and that in the meantime he should read his Bible to see what produces this genuine faith, unlike all he'd met before. He was so far out of the way, without transport, that I couldn't even easily think of ways to connect him to a local Bible-teaching church in our few minutes together. And with that, he walked off into the darkness, slamming the car door behind him, after briefly asking my name.

## Winks across the dance floor

What was I to make of this? Such travel experiences give me the shivers. They scream to me of God. But perhaps there's even better news than this experience screaming to me: the Bible seems to suggest it is only God whispering. In Luke 10, the seventy-two disciples arrive back from a mini-mission they've been on, and they're excited with what they've experienced.

'Even the demons submit to us in your name!' (Luke 10:17)

What is Jesus' reply? He tells them he's also seen incredible things in terms of evil defeated, but then goes on immediately to say:

'Do not rejoice that the spirits submit to you, but rejoice that your names are written in heaven' (Luke 10:20).

For some reason, he turns their attention away from the incredible spiritual experience they've just had to more concrete realities: whether they have received salvation or not.

And so, being overawed simply with the hitchhiker coincidence on the road, and being consumed by seeking more of those moments, would be to miss the point completely. It would be like enjoying standing beside the road sign to somewhere, when you could be at the place itself. Or like having your heart thrilled by the wink across the dance floor from someone you really like the look of. But to fantasize based on that would be missing out. Why not get to see whether you've interpreted that wink right, and whether it could become something more?

### Good, better, best: finding something more

St Augustine wrote:

> *Maior liber noster orbis terrarum est; in eo lego completum, quod in libro dei lego promissum.* (Our great book is the entire world; what I read as promised in the book of God I read fulfilled in it (the world).)[6]

Psalm 19 puts this relationship between God's word and God's world similarly:

> The heavens declare the glory of God;
>> the skies proclaim the work of his hands.
> Day after day they pour forth speech;
>> night after night they reveal knowledge.
> They have no speech, they use no words;
>> no sound is heard from them.
> Yet their voice goes out into all the earth,
>> their words to the ends of the world.
> In the heavens God has pitched a tent for the sun.
>> It is like a bridegroom coming out of his chamber,
>> like a champion rejoicing to run his course.
> It rises at one end of the heavens
>> and makes its circuit to the other;
>> nothing is deprived of its warmth.

The law of the LORD is perfect,
refreshing the soul.
The statutes of the LORD are trustworthy,
making wise the simple.
The precepts of the LORD are right,
giving joy to the heart.
The commands of the LORD are radiant,
giving light to the eyes . . .

They are more precious than gold,
than much pure gold;
they are sweeter than honey,
than honey from the honeycomb.
By them your servant is warned;
in keeping them there is great reward.

And in the New Testament:

For since the creation of the world God's invisible qualities –
his eternal power and divine nature – have been clearly seen,
being understood from what has been made, so that people
are without excuse.
(Romans 1:20)

So, where do our travels fit into all this? Well, this world and our experience of it display God's eternal power and divine nature quite clearly. They pour forth speech, even without words.

The world screams of a Maker but, yet far more heart-warmingly, clearer and sweeter, it speaks of it from God's law (Scripture).

When we come to his words, we meet his Son in the intimate whispers of the Holy Spirit. We meet God face to face in all his glory, walking off the pages of the Scriptures. It's where meeting the Inventor of travel is the experience of a lifetime, one that no amount of travel could ever afford to give you. And that's why, no matter what culture of person I meet, I try either orally or physically to get them engaging with some of the clearest parts of the Bible.[7] For my Japanese friends, that sometimes means turning to a part of the Bible they relate to well: Ecclesiastes and Proverbs. For my Western sceptical friends, it's often the eyewitness accounts of Jesus' life. As for my Muslim friends, they love the stories of the prophets, particularly the ones they know of and have heard before in some variation.

### *From Middle Eastern market to home*

As we run together for our boat now, I hope we're more aware of the lenses we're wearing, and how impossible it is to take them off. Regardless, we can look back on our time in the Middle East with fondness, as we remember not only the funny clashes of culture but, overwhelmingly, how God still speaks into every culture so clearly despite our lenses. This will be a good jetty to launch from as we head towards the hardest part of our travels. For now, though, let's lie back and enjoy the sunset on board as we sail off into the night.

## Questions for the ride

- Was this the first time you thought about guilt–innocence and shame–honour cultures? If so, what struck you most about them?
- Where does your culture sit on this scale? Perhaps if you're not sure, you could do some research on <www.theculturetest.com>.
- What other lenses do you see through? Think of your socio-economic class, your gender, your political allegiances or your theological background. Why not spend thirty days reading the Bible through lenses not your own? If you find that hard to do, why not grab a Christian book written by someone from a different cultural background from you and see what surprises you?
- In what ways do you undermine Scripture by letting your experience of travel, church or life dictate to you the way things are?

### Prayer

Incomprehensible King of kings,
without your kindness to us in revealing yourself,
we would be as Hamlet searching for Shakespeare
in the play he was created for.
But we thank you that you have stepped into
the play, and that you've spoken with us and
made yourself clearly known.
We thank you that the Infinite confined
himself to show up on our doorstep and
walk among us.

We are sorry when we satisfy ourselves with the
tiny glimpses of you, and now we cast ourselves down
in front of Jesus and his words and want to shape
our lives and travels by them.
We pray that even our doubts would cause our faith
to rise, as we see your Lordship over every nation,
culture and lens, and come to delight more and more
in the truth and beauty of the Lord Jesus Christ
as a result of our travels.
In his name,
Amen.

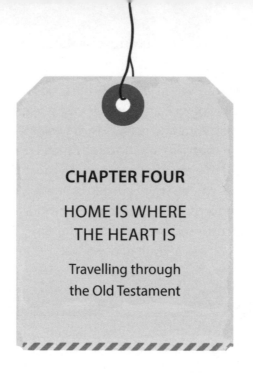

**CHAPTER FOUR**

**HOME IS WHERE THE HEART IS**

Travelling through the Old Testament

It's a funny thing coming home. Nothing changes.
Everything feels the same, looks the same, even smells
the same. You realize that what has changed is you.
(Eric Roth, adapting F. Scott Fitzgerald)[1]

*Níl aon tinteán mar do thinteán féin.*
There's no place like home.
(Irish)

***Destination***: Unknown
***Weather***: Cold and dank with glowering skies
***Company***: Crowds of people but no-one in particular

I first met Jack when my sister dropped me a message to ask
whether I'd host him in my living room as a Couchsurfer. He was
everything in a person that I would usually struggle to host, but

since she had asked I thought she'd have her reasons. Jack, originally from across the Atlantic, had been travelling virtually non-stop for five years, and within a few minutes of his arrival I'd been given the introduction to the five years' worth of stories that were to follow. But as he was able to hold us captive with stories, and he arrived bearing gifts and willing to lend a hand in the house, we relaxed and decided that running with it was best for one evening.

Apparently, we showed a little too much attention though, as three nights later Jack's stories could still be heard roaring from the kitchen table as he chatted away to anyone who'd be entertained.

Three years later I got a phone call from Jack. He was back in Ireland and wondered whether he could stay the night. But from the moment he walked through the door I could tell this was a very different Jack. His second question was about what alcoholic beverages we had in the house. And it wasn't long before old travel stories were replaced by stories of woe about how everyone had forsaken him, how all of life was going wrong, and how he'd settle down soon as a result. He was just finding out where. But at the rate he used our house resources, and with his failure to ask a single question to any of us about our lives, I guessed he was going to find this settling-down phase hard, even if he claimed to know everyone in the world.

Six months later he was back one final time, this time an absolute ruin. Picked up from the pub at 11 a.m., he assured me he wasn't addicted to alcohol. He was on crutches and couldn't find anyone to host him. Work was going to be a hard ask when he was in such a state. Could he stay the night? My housemates said no.

Wandering, done to its extreme, has this tragic effect on people. This prodigal son was ready to return home, but for a while he'd forgotten where home was or who could even be family. Was not being on the road the most desired thing he could imagine?

## *No place like home*

It's not just Jack who struggles to know where home is any more. Having lived in two cultures so far, and a third place that was a mix of the two, I feel the tug of both cultures on my life and that there are enough people in my life already too! Considering embracing a life of overseas mission is daunting. Culturally, it's hard enough balancing two cultures already, and frankly it's impossible to think I could fit any more people into my life without losing some who are very dear to me.

The phenomenon of the 'third-culture kid' (TCK) is increasingly common in today's nomadic, international world: a parent from one culture, another parent from a second culture, and the child feeling like they're stranded as a mixture of those and wherever they grew up!

Home is a funny concept.

On one TV show, ten members of the public, acting as fugitives, are let loose around the UK and given twenty-five days to evade capture by a team of surveillance experts, with a cash prize of £100,000 at stake. What amused me over the course of three series was the huge proportion of the thirty contestants all seeking to go home at some point during those days on the run, despite how obvious this would be to the surveillance team.

Whether it is family, friends, familiarity or something else, we're all drawn back to a concept of home.

And that's always been the case, right from the start. The Bible is a story of God calling a people from the nations, bringing them under his loving rule and moving them towards his Promised Land. There's a desire for a place we can truly call home. There's a desire to find a people we can feel at home with. And there's a finding of ourselves as we travel along the road. In that way, the Bible is one big travel journey, albeit not necessarily one that you or I would recognize from our pleasure travels.

See if you can spot some of the themes above as we take a tour together of ten top destinations in the Old Testament. As we go, we'll start to see a little of God's panorama of travel.

### *Ten top Old Testament travel destinations*

*Destination*: Unknown
*Mode of transport*: Cruising on a boat
*Company*: Noah, his wife, small family circle
and every animal imaginable under the sun

Our motorboat in Cork harbour is passing a giant cruise liner docked nearby with several thousand tourists on board, about to head across the Atlantic for America. From not far away, over a hundred years ago, the now-infamous *Titanic* was in a similar position, with excited passengers wanting to be on this ship, one of the largest and finest of its time. Looking up at it from below reminds me of a boat built by one of the earliest biblical travellers: Noah (Genesis 6).

At a time when people were building a name for themselves, Noah and his family appear instead as figures looking to a name beyond themselves: God's name, hearing his words. We see them in Genesis embarking on the seemingly hilarious project of building a boat in a place with little water, and then entering through a door to where they would be safe from the floods of judgment. They must have been the most mocked travellers ever!

But the flood does come, and their project is well and truly vindicated. When God eventually lets the flood waters recede, it is Noah and his descendants with whom he freely establishes a covenant (or contract), something so visibly gracious given what Noah goes on to do later in the chapter. Noah may have had home and heritage destroyed, but he is found safe in a new place of rest, outside the judgment of God, having trusted God's words (Hebrews 11:7).

This would be a metaphorical home better than any other. For those in the world travelling because they've been displaced, he is a trailblazer for being content to find home away from physical possessions and any sense of belonging, in the safety of following God, no matter what that might mean.

*Destination*: Canaan (from Haran)
*Mode of transport*: By animal and on foot
*Company*: Abram, his descendants, family and servants

Planning a route and what actually happens are always two completely different things for me. With map open, I think I'll happily hop from place to place with no hiccups and everything going smoothly. But reality isn't like that. Either some spontaneous interactions are too good to leave, or a stunning spot that I didn't expect shows up irresistibly on the horizon! I'm not the only one apparently.

Abram and his wife and family were travellers by command of God (Genesis 11 onwards). He'd commanded his dad to go to Canaan, but they'd only made it as far as Haran before they settled. The command to Abram is to go and complete the journey to a land that could be called 'home', provided by God. In a world that didn't follow God, Abram appears as a figure who had faith in him and his words. We see him here in Genesis confronted with the news that his old, old wife Sarai will give birth, and that offspring greater in number than the grains of sand on the seashore or the stars in the sky will come through her. Building a boat in a barren land nearly becomes more believable than this!

Now God gives a gracious covenant despite their doubts, and despite Sarai, who would have been feeling full of shame for not having produced offspring in her culture at that time.

God's covenant promise with a people whom he would draw to himself from all nations was a long-haul plan that would involve some unwanted travel for four hundred years into Egypt. But the lesson of the promise? God would be in control, despite what it looked like. He would be their great reward, going before them, preparing them for their new home. The nations were in his hand, and he had a plan that wouldn't be thwarted. Coming home would all be about belonging to a people. When they were there, it would feel just like home.

This is worth bearing in mind as we travel, especially when it all seemingly goes wrong and plans don't work out, or we experience illness, theft or other darker sides of life. Does this mean that God's promises aren't true? Not at all!

*Destination*: A well crawl
*Mode of transport*: By animal and on foot
*Company*: Abraham, Isaac's servant, Jacob, Moses, and servants (not all at once, though)

Visiting countries that don't have accessible water supplies is something I haven't yet got used to. Staying in a house in the middle of an African market, I asked the family where the shower was for the morning.

'Just go out the door, take a right, take the second street on the left, walk down five doors and give the door a knock. The person who opens the door will know why you're there, and they'll give you a scrub and make sure you're dry afterwards.'

Needless to say, I didn't have the courage to shower the next morning! But for those who do not even have water to drink, the luxury of choice is not great. Miles to walk for some, just to find a place where they can get water.

So, here we are sitting by a well (Genesis 24). Beside us is Abraham's servant. He's travelled miles to find this spot, and it's a divinely ordained dating spot at that! His master didn't fancy his son marrying any of the Canaanites, not because of their looks, but because of whom they worshipped and followed in life – they didn't worship the living God. So, in order to be faithful, after reaching the spot, the servant asks God to cause the woman he should choose to fulfil certain conditions.

A while later she arrived, doing the very things that were God's signs that she was the right woman: not just offering a drink (unusual), but offering to water all his camels too (a huge job!). And back he goes to her place . . . and voilà.

Come with me to the next well . . .
One generation (five chapters) later and we're sitting by *another* well with some shepherds, when along comes Jacob.

'How's it going, boy?'
'Ah, grand – have you seen my mother's brother around in your home town recently?'
'Well, yes, and here comes his daughter.'

And so, off goes Jacob back to Rachel's place to meet his mother's brother. And again! Another well-made match. (Sorry!)

And lest two of the central figures of Jewish history weren't enough, we'll add on a third well for good measure. This time we're sitting around and, as so often happens, the female shepherds get hounded by their male counterparts (Exodus 2). The men won't let the women near the water troughs at the well. But, wait, what's this? In storms the saviour of the day – Moses – to push them back and allow the women to access water for their needs. The women return early to their father, he's surprised and asks them why they're early, and they tell of their great hero. And you guessed it, Moses marries one of this chap's daughters. Voilà, number three!

I could go on. You see, wells were pretty loaded locations in Israelite stories, as often they were social hubs out of necessity. But in all of these cases, the need to find a wife for someone in a land that didn't have much choice was key. There wasn't a chance they'd marry and raise a family with someone who didn't see eye to eye with them in how to reach out intention- ally to the nations and live distinctly in God's big plan. And so, they travelled.

I'm not sure of the relevance of this exactly, given that marriage works very differently in our culture from theirs, but when fleeting mad thoughts come into our heads about getting off with someone while we're travelling (no-one will see, right?), we'd do well to have this much determined level-headedness as we intentionally seek a life partner among God's people (that is, if we intend to marry at all). 'Home' is to be a place where like-minded people help each other to thrive in life together.

For those living in countries with small numbers of Christians, or for those who feel they have niche callings to unengaged people groups or other similarly unlikely areas, this may present challenges. But as someone who is in both of these positions, I can encourage you that God is faithful, and will help us as we strive for godly contentment in a world that constantly cries out 'more!'

***Destination***: The Desert
***Mode of transport***: By animal and on foot
***Company***: The whole of Israel (plus extras)

Sometimes getting the big picture is very different from seeing something up close. I remember standing on top of some of Europe's tallest cliffs and thinking that really they weren't anything amazing. Until I zoomed in with my camera on a large sea bird wheeling around in the air a hundred metres below, and saw just how small it was.

Oh.

A moment of realization.

And so it is with desert wandering. If you've never been in a desert, it's hard fully to appreciate how easy it is to 'grumble like an Israelite' (see nearly every chapter in Numbers).

When you've spent even one night in the desert in a pop-up tent, or walked a gruelling day without seeing anything but sand all around you, or driven a day in a car that isn't designed for desert driving and is fast running out of petrol (so much so that you turn off the air conditioning, just to preserve fuel), then you can start to imagine what walking seemingly purposeless days on end must have been like for the Israelites.

Discipline for continually doubting God's good purposes, even after he had rescued them from slavery in special ways, came hand in hand with providing for them and having enabled them to evade local warrior populations who would have slaughtered them if they'd escaped Egypt in other directions (Exodus 13:17–18). For forty years they wandered the desert, until the next generation were prepared to accept that God *might just* have a future for them, matching their past story of rescue.

And so it is with us: we'd do well continually to persuade our hearts of the goodness of God and not abandon hope, even if we go through excruciating times that cloud our vision. God's glory, our good and everything else that is promised to happen in this world may not seem to be positive for us at the time. But seeing the bigger travel narrative of the past will persuade us that they still can be, are and will be, despite how it may seem. Our journey to our spiritual 'home' as citizens of heaven will have lots of rocky moments. But let's not lose heart or perspective.

*Destination*: The festival
*Mode of transport*: By animal and on foot
*Company*: The faithful of Israel, able to travel (plus extras)

We all have them. The 'together' moments. The ecstasy of experiencing something in a large number. Whether you're a music festival junkie, or whatever it is that makes you want to travel to be with others, there's no doubt something special occurs when we find ourselves in big crowds.

This is why many people plan their travels to coincide with the big festivals. Whether it's catching New Year with the crowds in

Edinburgh, the beach parties of the Festival of 'San Juan' in Spain or the raves all night long on Thai beaches with the sun setting, we love it.

And it's not just those liberal twenty-something-year-olds who do festivals and 'group experiences'. No, head up to the tranquillity of the Western Isles of Scotland and you'll find a completely different, yet still spine-tingling, experience in a religious community there.

The Free Church of Scotland holds a special communion celebration of Jesus' death and resurrection a couple of times a year. And to prepare themselves and remember the importance of the latter, they meet for one week, every night of the week, to still their hearts and confess their shamefulness before the God they serve, both as individuals and as a community. In seeing more of their shame and imperfection, they rejoice more at the end of the week in the perfect solution that removes this shame for ever.

On a cold winter evening you'll find them packing into homes of local believers that weren't ever meant to host that number. And you won't be there long before haunting a-cappella melodies will start from the Bible's song book (the Psalms), pointing people to humanity's persistent shame, and to the solution. Three- or even four-part harmonies will not be out of place, and all singers are welcomed, regardless of ability. It's beautiful! The tears welled in my eyes as I listened. The memories will last a long time.

But what are these songs they're singing? Ancient songs from many thousands of years ago, preserved (but rearranged close to the time) in historical records to give us a glimpse of the festival tunes that would have been known by everyone – the hits that lasted down the years.

And some I've been studying recently are songs that would have been put together for the road. Songs for travel, for when Jewish people were setting out for the big religious festivals in Jerusalem where their temple was located. They felt the buzz of the coming festival and of being with likeminded people for a change (Psalm 120). Everyone was on the road, but the roads weren't as easy as ours.

The hills were to be feared, when the songwriter turns his eyes to them (Psalm 121). They were like the Jericho road that the good Samaritan walked. Are there gangs lurking behind the next rock? What will walking in the heat of the sun do to us? Or what about when the sun sets and casts chilling shadows over the hills?

Together, when the people get to the festival, they will glimpse what they long for – true peace between people with whom they are united (Psalm 122). That will be fully known in the future, in a 'Jerusalem' that won't be an Israeli capital city, in a 'Zion' that will be as if God is the towering mountains of safety (and not of fear) around them (Psalm 125), protecting them from evil people (Psalm 124).

This festival will help us send postcards home, reminding everyone across the world what God has done, even when it's hard to see (Psalm 126). These festivals will remind us there's something bigger than ourselves, something that we should give even our very offspring to honour (Psalm 127).

And I could go on. Psalms 133 and 134 seem to speak of an arrival into the ecstasy of the festival – no longer being on the road. God's people are doing what they were made for: worshipping God together. And it feels like home, doing this in God's presence: where they were made for. Home!

The psalms are marked in the ancient manuscripts as the 'Songs of Ascents' (Psalms 120–134), and they come to life when you remember the context of the traveller on the hard road up to the festival. As I've spent hours on the road with work, I've been transformed by various musical groups who've helped me learn the psalms, meditate upon them and contextualize them to the world we live in today.

And even when I'm travelling light I have my phone with three 'apps' for each day: my Bible app (with reading plan), my prayer diary app, and my hymns and songs app. A perfect trio in my pocket, even for when I'm flying with hand luggage only!

*Destination*: King Solomon's Palace in Israel
*Mode of transport*: Convoy of animals and servants
*Company*: Queen of Sheba and attendants[2]

What makes you travel? Is there ever a person, a celebrity or someone in the media who catches your attention and compels you to explore more about them? More of us travel for other people than we think, if you include music gigs, sports matches, comedians and celebrities. But when you meet the person face to face, would you remain as in awe of them as you were before?

Here the queen of a far-off land comes to explore the wisdom of a rule given by the gracious hand of God. Even the visitors recognize something of this, and many are in awe of such wisdom. But for Solomon, wise as he is, such wisdom goes to his head, as riches and wives become his focus, and his end is that of one who chases after other gods. The ultimate 'home', therefore, will not be found in belonging to the safety of Solomon's kingly rule, but under the rule of a wiser Ruler to come, that of Christ.

But such a fascination to travel miles to study under someone respected still goes on every year, and is a huge reason why many travel today. International students at universities and colleges are highly profitable for governments, and study years abroad or overseas degrees are very common.

Students come to the 'Christian West' thinking that everything they see is pure religion, good and faithful to what Christ said. But, instead, they see worship of self, material wealth and a lifestyle to match, and partnerships with things that seem very unchristian indeed.

And yet, just like in the book of Acts, today we see that a great percentage of those who come to faith are in a foreign setting! Travelling does something to you that makes you think outside the current confines of your world view, or it can do, as we saw earlier.

And so, still teams of Christians all over the world (like the one mentioned by Seamus earlier) set up weekly community café spaces to 'welcome the foreigner', and in doing so they model such beautiful, thoughtful community that many start to ask questions and discuss some of the deep longings of their cultures and lives. Similarly, hospitality programmes run by local churches give people a 'home away from home', and allow students to meet those from local backgrounds who aren't their age or generation. For the helpers or hosts, this is a rich experience too, learning without moving from their own doorstep, and getting a chance to be used as God shapes the nations with his voice, using their frail arms and words. Many have come to experience the home that Christ's kingly rule offers through the haven of rest inside the doors of Christian community.

Ahmed (a Saudi Royal) was in Ireland for his year abroad. Here's his story:

I'd been told back home to watch out for the ungodly Christians who worship three gods: drink and party like there's no god, and having sex as if they are god. I got off the plane prepared for this Christian country, and when my university had arranged for me to be picked up at the airport and taken to my halls of residence, I was nervous when my driver said he was a Christian, but I said nothing.

Later on I secretly accepted that I would go to this person's home, although I knew I should not eat their unclean food or get too close to the females in the house, who seemed to have no problem in welcoming me, a little too warmly.

As my year went on, I started to learn the difference between those who follow Jesus and most of the people here who don't at all. I started to doubt what I'd been told about Christians back home. And when I doubted that, I also started to question other things. The warmth and community of diverse people at the international café really helped me, and soon I was finding the spiritual discussions on the life of the prophets to be a weekly thing I would do with a friend there.

I'm very thankful for these Christians now. I can see they are good religious people who apply their faith to their studies more than I have ever done. This has challenged me.

**Destination**: Nineveh
**Mode of transport**: By boat, on foot or otherwise
**Company**: Jonah and anyone who would help him escape

It's the perfect getaway. If you have had to bear preachy, conservative folk breathing down your neck, whether that be family, friends or just the culture around you, you'll know what I mean!

Getting away from people who enforce their thoughts and narrow ways of living on you, and escaping into the utter wilds and freedom is an epic feeling. But even if you're not escaping anything other than the mundane things of life, it's still fabulous.

Going wherever.

Doing things whenever.

Meeting anyone you want along the way.

The world is your playground!

Now, feeling bitter about such a religious, conservative culture may not be a bad thing (some religion, making itself known or felt as primarily 'do nots', is not true religion at all). But, in this story, the bitterness of our friend Jonah is far from justified (though certainly understandable).

Jonah has decided that the people to whom he was asked to bring the bad news about God's judgment and the good news about God's rescue are not worthy of it. This was a fairly natural feeling, given the horrors present in surrounding cultures at the time, even if we're always quick to forget our own failings and how God dealt with them (in grace).

And so, not understanding the irony of refusing this mission, he does a runner in precisely the other direction, away from Nineveh. He goes to the port of Joppa, jumps on a ship going to Tarshish and heads off travelling. It's the natural reaction when we don't want to face the music and dance.

But he's missed one crucial thing. He can't hide from God. As God's children, we can't hide from God. There are no places devoid of God. And no places that God is more inclined to hang out in than others. God's home is everywhere he is. The psalmist wrote of the beauty of that thought:

> You have searched me, LORD,
>     and you know me.
> You know when I sit and when I rise;
>     you perceive my thoughts from afar.
> You discern my going out and my lying down;
>     you are familiar with all my ways . . .

You hem me in behind and before,
    and you lay your hand upon me . . .

Where can I go from your Spirit?
    Where can I flee from your presence?
If I go up to the heavens, you are there;
    if I make my bed in the depths, you are there.
If I rise on the wings of the dawn,
    if I settle on the far side of the sea,
even there your hand will guide me,
    your right hand will hold me fast.
(Psalm 139:1–3, 5, 7–10)

Amazing knowledge! But equally, those who don't follow God can't run from his judgment either (Amos 9:1–6). The justice that we yearn for against evil will one day happen:

I saw the Lord standing by the altar, and he said:

'Strike the tops of the pillars
    so that the thresholds shake.
Bring them down on the heads of all the people;
    those who are left I will kill with the sword.
Not one will get away,
    none will escape.
Though they dig down to the depths below,
    from there my hand will take them.
Though they climb up to the heavens above,
    from there I will bring them down.
Though they hide themselves on the top of Carmel,
    there I will hunt them down and seize them.

Though they hide from my eyes at the bottom of the sea,
   there I will command the serpent to bite them.
Though they are driven into exile by their enemies,
   there I will command the sword to slay them.

'I will keep my eye on them
   for harm and not for good.'
(Amos 9:1–4)

It is fearful imagery.

There is no escape from God.

## *Running away*

And that's what I found one evening when I was back again hosting Couchsurfers with my housemates. Two central European students were looking for accommodation, and we said we'd take them in for the evening. We ate together and then headed for the pub (the cultural meeting place in our culture, not connected to excessive drinking, despite the Irish reputation), to experience some live traditional Irish music.

We chatted for hours, hearing of their travels, exchanging cultural nuggets of wisdom and asking questions, both at surface and at deeper levels. And as we headed back to the house, the craic was at such good levels that we stuck our favourite music on in the kitchen, put on the kettle for some tea and kept chatting for hours. It was only when one of them went to go to the toilet that he noticed a stack of John's Gospels that I'd accidentally left out after a week's work.

'Why on earth do you live with Christians?' he asked, oblivious to the fact that I was one myself.

'Why not?' I replied. 'Are there things that you disagree about or find repulsive about living with them?'

And so the conversation took a strange turn for the next hour, as one of them broke down in tears when he found out I was a Christian. He'd been raised in an evangelical home (what are the chances?), but had found it so strict on things like alcohol, their particular views of creation, their lack of appreciation for the arts – he now made clothing for a living – and many other things, that his view of Jesus deteriorated as he experienced this evangelical community that made him so bitter. He'd never known a Christian who would sit in a pub with him, and later listen to his deep questions about the 'hows' of creation and wrestle with him about how to be a Christian in the arts world.

'Maybe I should go back to Jesus and see what he's like,' was his conclusion to this epic conversation, while his friend just sat observing and drinking it all in.

Not all conversations go like this with 'prodigal' travellers. I mean, I could tell of just as many prodigals who, although all the reasons that caused them not to believe are removed, still refuse to engage when it comes to Jesus. The fear of the supposed straitjacket of having him as Lord of their travels keeps many searching to find who they are *outside* of him, until they see what type of 'home' they are missing out on: that it's called love, and that it is the most 'liberating freedom-loss'[3] of all time. And Jesus is the fountain of it.

***Destination***: Israel
***Mode of transport***: On foot
***Company***: Ruth, Naomi and Orpah

In recent weeks I've spent time with refugees fortunate enough to have come to Ireland as Syrian migrants through the government systems. They didn't risk life and limb to cross oceans in tiny inflatables, but they did watch their homes being destroyed bit by bit in a mass genocide that has scarred several generations mentally, emotionally and physically. And so they travelled . . .

Sitting there trying not to let their migrant status mean I would treat them as subhuman in a one-way relationship, my mind wandered to a story of economic migrants of old.

A famine happens in ancient Israel and Judah, and some people leave for Moab to find food. It's a time when everyone was doing what was right in their own eyes, and few cared for God and his ways and purposes. Whether the famine was because of disobedience to God (causal connections in that time in Israel were more usual in their covenant with God), or whether they were showing a lack of faith by moving, is not mine to know or say.

But somehow, a vulnerable woman (oppressed as women were in their society) finds her way along the road, with her mother-in-law and sister-in-law. All three women's husbands had died and they were without inheritance, during a famine, having just walked about a hundred miles by foot (a week perhaps?). Two of the women decide to head back to Israel (one of them a foreign Moabite) as things were easing up with the famine.

Thankfully, unlike other ancient Near Eastern cultures, Israel's laws allowed for a 'kinsman-redeemer' who would be responsible for providing in such situations, and taking such vulnerable people under his wing, should they desire.

In this case, instead of this figure taking responsibility, another man steps in who goes out of his way to lavish far more on these women than is required by law, refuses to abuse his power and sleep with the women, and asks for permission from the closer relative to take care of them.

It's a powerful story of immigration, the death of loved ones, famine, honour and romance, all in four short chapters.

And it's a story of migrants that is meant to point forward to a greater reality of what is still to come. A Redeemer (someone who will 'buy back') coming to rescue humanity from the circumstances it has got itself into, and the conscious and subconscious things, seemingly moral and not-so-moral, that we prostrate ourselves before. This Redeemer will come when there's no other way out, and with grace and kindness will lavish on us far more than just contractual obedience.

As we face the migrant crisis, the factors that create it and our selfish hearts that exacerbate it, may it make us long for a Redeemer like this! But it also reminds us that God calls the outsider from the nations – some of the least expected from every people group in the world – into his family.

Here's a story that should challenge and push us outwards to the nations and to those we consider the 'least' among them, especially as our pleasure vessels pass those deathly dinghies full of those who may not survive another day.

**Destination**: Mount Carmel
**Mode of transport**: On foot
**Company**: Elijah and the prophets of Baal

Sometimes we come across people who worship gods strangely absent from this world. Their home seems to be in some ethereal realm. Like absentee landlords, their existence is something we philosophize about and just hope we might be right. Many Irish will pray to an 'old man' whom they hope is up in the sky, and get very religious when death and other horrible things happen.

And such accusations can have some leverage. Even the prophet Elijah in Old Testament times was recorded as challenging the other prophets in a fire duel, saying about their god:

'Shout louder! Surely he is a god! Perhaps he is deep in thought, or busy, or travelling. Maybe he is sleeping and must be awakened' (1 Kings 18:27).

Would we want a god who enjoys travel? Well, not in this way, in the sense of not always showing up. We already have plenty of choices of religions with absentee landlord gods, leaving us saying with Bertrand Russell (one of the UK's most famous philosophers and atheists), 'Not enough evidence god, not enough evidence',[4] when asked to believe in them. By contrast, we have a God who travels right to our doorstep and shows up to make his home among us.

**Destination**: Israel
**Mode of transport**: On horseback
**Company**: Raiders from other nations

Throughout the Scriptures God was extremely gracious to the world, and in particular to his people. Although we read from John 1 that 'the law was given through Moses; grace and truth came through Jesus Christ', this doesn't mean that grace was unknown in the old covenant. In fact, the old covenant was in itself a covenant of grace, as we've briefly seen from the travellers we've met so far.

So, why do we get raiding parties that seem to be divinely allowed?

Well, precisely because of what we've seen elsewhere. Grace and judgment often go together. It is God's grace that sends raiding parties to judge unfaithful people, to call them back to his way of human flourishing:

'I brought you up out of Egypt and led you into the land that I swore to give to your ancestors. I said, "I will never break my covenant with you, and you shall not make a covenant with the people of this land, but you shall break down their altars." Yet you have disobeyed me. Why have you done this? And I have also said, "I will not drive them out before you; they will become traps for you, and their gods will become snares to you."'

When the angel of the Lord had spoken these things to all the Israelites, the people wept aloud, and they called that place Bokim. There they offered sacrifices to the Lord.

(Judges 2:1–5)

One generation and five verses later we read:

After that whole generation had been gathered to their ancestors, another generation grew up who knew neither the Lord nor what he had done for Israel. Then the Israelites did evil in the eyes of the Lord and served the Baals. They forsook the Lord, the God of their ancestors, who had brought them out of Egypt. They followed and worshipped various gods of the peoples around them. They aroused the Lord's anger because they forsook him and served Baal and the Ashtoreths. In his anger against Israel the Lord gave them into the hands of raiders who plundered them. He sold them into the hands of their enemies all around, whom they were no longer able to resist. Whenever Israel went out to fight, the hand of the Lord was against them to defeat them, just as he had sworn to them. They were in great distress.

(Judges 2:10–15)

And so, continually, although God provided local rescuers in different parts of the country despite their disobedience, the people soon forgot his gracious provision and went back to their own ways. The stories of the judges are not primarily meant to point us to amazing people whom we should emulate, but rather to a gracious God who used a temporary means of grace to stave off those raiding parties that were the source of judgment. And so it is when we think too much about making this world our home – we're quickly reminded by circumstances outside of our control that we are not meant to get too comfy.[5]

## *Takeaways from our Old Testament travel*

So, coming to the end of our grand tour of Old Testament travellers and destinations, what are we to make of it all? We've seen quite a mixed bag of travels, which could so easily be seen as having nothing to do with each other! But, uniting them all in their great diversity, we've seen that God's people have stumbled time and time again, yet God has been faithful to his covenant promises to gather to himself a people who belong, under his loving authority, as they've travelled onwards towards their eventual home. Even that hasn't gone smoothly, and they await a 'home' to come, far beyond what they've experienced so far.

As the authors' intentions weren't to speak primarily about pleasure travel or similar, it's hard to get a feel from the Old Testament of how we're to travel in this way. The topic is clear by its absence, rather than by its presence, yet many principles are clear.

Before we go off on the second half of our travels through the Scriptures, and this time island-hop around some paradise Pacific Islands, which can be our backdrop, let's stop and thank God for what we have seen so far.

### Questions for the road

- Can you think of other Old Testament travelling stories that we've missed out? What do they teach us about God and his eternal home, but also about our travels?

- How has seeing these patterns of faith, unbelief, grace and judgment in Scripture helped you have confidence in the God of history who has travelled with his people so faithfully?
- What can we tell from the absence of pleasure travels in the Old Testament?
- What do we learn about our ultimate goal as we travel?
  - Where is it?
  - Who is it with?
  - What does that haven of safety and authority look like?

### Prayer

God of history,
you are faithful to your gracious promises
to your travelling people.
What you've said comes to pass,
and your purposes prevail.
As we've seen you build yourself a people from
the nations, help us to travel with that in mind.
As we've seen you lead your people towards a home,
help us to yearn for that home.
And as we've seen your good, loving rule,
help us to appreciate how you treat your children
as we travel to achieve your purposes in this world.
In the ambiguity of the travel of old,
help us to understand the principles.
Amen

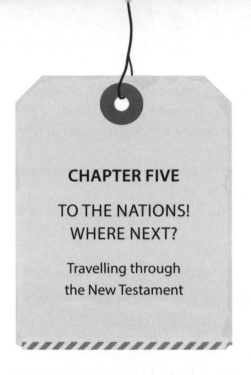

## CHAPTER FIVE

## TO THE NATIONS! WHERE NEXT?

Travelling through
the New Testament

And if travel is like love, it is, in the end,
mostly because it's a heightened state of awareness,
in which we are mindful, receptive, undimmed by familiarity
and ready to be transformed. That is why the best trips,
like the best love affairs, never really end.
(Pico Iyer)[1]

Our destinations this time aren't from the Bible narrative itself, but colourful backdrops for exciting themes that I'll mull over in my hammock. But, first, let's rewind the history of our general location, Vanuatu . . .

John G. Paton was a missionary from Scotland, sent by his church to the New Hebrides in the Pacific Islands in 1858. There he faced a wild bunch of cannibals who practised infanticide and killed widows so that they could go and serve their husbands in the afterlife. They were a people gripped by fear, who made frequent attempts to get rid of John, despite his passion to empower them in business and creativity, and his campaign against colonial slavery and suchlike. Sadly, his wife and child were to die from a fever soon after arriving on the islands.

Although John and others mobilized the people to reach their fellow islanders with the good news of Jesus, and thousands of them came to faith as a result, the gospel still takes time to establish convictions and root itself in a culture. And so it was, 150 years later, that one of the first-ever missionaries was sent by the church of Vanuatu (previously the New Hebrides) to an unreached people group in Africa.

Others had gone to more easily reached shores, including their own. But this was one of the first missionaries to leave for parts flung far beyond their own. Today they are preparing to be involved in this work across the nations, and amid the messiness of life are rendering hilarious the claim that Christianity is a remnant of Western colonial days. They join thousands of others from non-Western countries, leaving with full hearts for places where Christ is not yet known.

As we explore the New Testament and see what it teaches us about travel, we'll get glimpses of how it compels us to respond in our own lives. We'll see more developed pictures of the 'home' that we've been promised already in our last chapter.

Jump on board as we island-hop around Vanuatu and hear the people tell us first-hand what they think.

*Island*: Efate, Port Vila, home to colourful market stalls offering produce and local handicrafts. A base for divers and visitors to Mele Cascades, a multi-tiered waterfall with rock pools in a rainforest
*Location*: My hammock
*Topic*: Encountering controversy as we travel

I walked in to my room at a rural youth hostel recently to find the other two occupants of said room, one lying on top of the other, and quite shocked that they had company (thankfully, not just me). At my appearing, they disappeared . . . off to find a place where they could make love undisturbed and, let's face it, probably in a more romantic setting than a shabby hostel dorm.

Travelling always lends itself to one-night stands and quick flings. But much as this is the case, while thinking (wrongly) that your sex goes unseen and without harm to anyone, I doubt if many people would go short-term travelling to find themselves a wife. You might move countries to where you deem the opposite sex will suit you better, yes, but not short-term travels! In fact, of those who have done this, most don't recommend the messiness of distance and culture at all.

I invite you to rejoin the well crawl that we started earlier – you'll remember from the last chapter that wells were pretty loaded locations in Israelite stories. Our final well is in the eyewitness account of Jesus' life in John 4 and seems to be little different at first glance.

## *Unlikely encounter*

Add to the history above the fact that men of Jesus' culture *did not* strike up conversations with women. If you go to the Middle East and do that, you'll realize just how inappropriate it is, even today. Add too the fact that this woman was of the opposite tribe or team. I've grown up with a great clash in my culture between Ireland and Britain, but this is far worse.

And to top it all off, Jesus is tired and travelling. I mean, have you ever been on the road for a while? When I'm travelling is normally the time I get my head down, read a book or sleep. I pity the person who tries to have any meaningful chat with me.

Enter stage right: the very least of the women from this 'other' tribe. In fact, so much the least that she's sufficiently scared of the snide remarks, abuse and shame from her past that she is making her way to the well at the hottest part of the day. If you've ever been in that part of the world, you'll know how stupid a thing that is to do. And so, the conversation starts – one to one.

'Can I have a drink?'

Any potential controversy dies away when Jesus makes it clear what he's after. He could have launched in to criticize her and heap judgment on her like everyone else (for she'd had five husbands). It wouldn't have taken much to make her feel really ashamed. But no, what does he say? He intrigues her by telling her that he can give eternally satisfying water. This living water has been a theme throughout the prophets . . . everyone knew that.[2]

She remembers from what she's been taught that even the best of wells couldn't have done that.

'What do you mean?' she asks.
'Bring your husband and come back.'

Gulp. There it is – the same shame moment.

Only, she *doesn't seem ashamed.* In fact, she seems more excited about finding out about this water, because the conversation keeps going. I don't know about you, but I shut down a conversation pretty quickly when I feel shame, or I babble on incessantly about something different and meaningless.

She's amazed at what this prophet knows. It's likely in her culture that the five men have treated her very badly in relationships and left her. Women didn't have much say in such situations, yet would still end up with a bad reputation as a result.

### Side-stepping difference

But putting that controversy behind, and also side-stepping questions of what outward religious identity he expresses, Jesus points to a day when everyone who worships in Spirit and truth will worship together at the same place – 'home'. It's another thing the Promised One would do according to the prophets of old – everyone knew that – unite the nations and bring a people home.[3]

And just when one bullet is dodged, the next happens ... In walk his mates, to find him chatting one to one at a controversial location, in the tiredness of the heat with a saucy woman. But such is the purity and holiness of Jesus that no-one asks any questions. They all know nothing has happened.

Such love travels far beyond gender boundaries

> cultural boundaries
> religious boundaries
> tiredness.

Such love travels to those perceived most sinful.

Such love gently helps this woman see her true state.

Such love so intrigues and woos her heart spiritually that her shame and conviction of sin are felt as nothing compared to the all-surpassing grace that flows and points her to a greater place to find joy: truly finding herself, by coming to the Messiah.

Such love.

Her response is not surprising, is it? She ecstatically tells others. Nor is it surprising, for that matter, that those who gathered around to listen to Jesus' words go away changed by them.

And with that in mind, on my travels I want to meet more of the travelling One who offers all-satisfying waters. And as I meet more of him, I hope to find more of myself and who I was created to be. And perhaps those on the road with me will do so too, through my words and those of others.

*Island*: Epi Island, place of snorkelling, swimming, coconut-covered hills – a little piece of heaven. What's not to like?
*Location*: My hammock
*Topic*: Travelling with Christ (the cross)

Often we find Jesus doing things that we either can't possibly replicate or shouldn't even try to do. It's one of the big questions of the Bible that we get wrong time and time again. And it's not always simple to know.

In the Gospels we find Christ travelling (and refusing to travel) for many reasons:

- He travels to this earth (incarnation).
- He travels to reach people who haven't heard the good news.
- He travels for religious feasts (John 7:1–10).
- He deliberately travels to controversial places (John 4).
- He travels to escape and rest (Mark 1:35; 3:13; 6:46).
- He sometimes travels to avoid danger, but sometimes into danger.
- He travels towards the cross (Mark 10:32, 33, 38; 11:1, 11, 15, 27; 12:1–12; 14:48–49; 15; John 2:4; 12:24).
- He leaves this earth (ascension).

And I'm sure we could go on. All of the above seem not only very intentional, but also very real and very human. Intentionality doesn't breed robots or predictable actions. And perhaps that's where my heart fails so often – I love to think I know best what other people should be doing with their lives, right down to their travels! But I don't. And I shouldn't be dogmatic. My intentional decisions need not be yours. But a Christ-centred way of travelling should be.

And this Christ-centred way of travelling will be a cross-centred way. To find ourselves and a promised home, we must travel via the cross and keep it in sight at all times. Throughout John's eyewitness account of Jesus' life there's a constant reference to his phrase, 'My time has not yet come.' As we'll see later, that's connected to his substitutionary death on the cross and his constant moving towards that goal: the original reason why he came. We'll see in the next chapter what implications this might have for the traveller.

*Island*: Ambrym Island, popular with hikers and campers.
You eat whatever your guide manages to catch . . .
but beware of the volcanoes
*Location*: My hammock
*Topics*: Travelling on Roman roads; Greek thought

I love learning on the road. It makes for far more inter-esting ways of engaging with history, for example, a subject I never warmed to as a kid. And when my work sends me to a conference with top European academics and university workers, I'm especially happy. Sitting in Rome, I've had a chance to look up what others once told me about Roman roads and the early Church. I read that the Roman Empire had over 120,000 km of long, straight, vast networks of road, for trade and to keep control of areas, and some of those roads still exist today.

### *When in Rome*

Certain things come to mind that would have assisted the fast-spreading of the news and message of Jesus:

- Trade routes were easy for travel and for carrying messages.
- Trade routes already crossed cultures, and people were used to passing on messages across the divides.
- The 'home' language of most of the Empire was probably Greek, and therefore most people would have understood it.
- The Empire was largely united and stable, which allowed for greater ease of spreading messages.

Now, of course, these are just factors in the spread of the gospel, as God often uses human means to work in this messy world. Doubtless, the power of the gospel to change lives, the zeal of early Christians and many other spiritual factors were primary considerations.

But when we look at parts of history when the gospel didn't spread as quickly, perhaps it's not *just* due to completely sinful reasons (or not at all due to these). We must bear in mind context too, and of course the God who is sovereign in bringing about context, as he builds his Church and calls us home.[4]

### *Finding yourself*

As well as Roman roads, Greek thought has played a huge part in influencing Christianity, either through the syncretism (mixing beliefs) of the time or, more often than not, the researchers who looked at biblical texts and assumed that the authors must be using terms in the same way as other locals had done.

Often I meet folk on my travels who say: 'Prayer, reading your Bible, going to church, telling others about Jesus and a few other things [my cheeky edit: not many] are great things to do. However, travelling for fun, taking time off, sleeping, having passions, playing sport, doing art, playing computer games and sex . . . well they're not so good.'

Why? 'Well, they're, erm, not as spiritual!'

Or so the thinking goes in *most* religions. The Islamic call to prayer reminds us that prayer is better than sleep. I struggle to have a *normal* human conversation with the Jehovah's Witnesses whom I meet, without hearing their scripted replies! And in forms of Buddhism we must try to escape this world and the trappings of physical reality. Even, sadly, some Christian preachers say that the 'real you' is just some soul part that will go to be with God for ever in some airy-fairy homeland in the sky.

But all these things will frustrate the traveller who is trying to find himself or herself, as according to them there is nothing here on earth of much value at all!

Why has this crept into Christianity?

## It's all Greek to me

Often called 'dualism' in theology and philosophy, this ancient belief that makes you feel guilty about doing fairly normal things, and does not look favourably on the fact that Christ is Lord over everything, lurks round the corner in many Christian circles. It stems more from Greek Platonic thought (from Plato) than from the Bible, but it profoundly shapes the way many of us think.

And when it comes to travel, it has done this too. As well as it being easier to brand something in life either 'good' or 'evil' because of the comfort of having easy black-and-white divides, dualism is also a reason why many rant against anyone who is perceived to travel much for the sheer joy of it, or even rest. According to those who think the material is bad, unless you are doing something for the sake of 'souls', then it is worthless. Perhaps it's not often directly expressed in such terms, but implicitly many will think this way.

In fact, in some ways this even goes beyond a Platonic divide to a Gnostic heresy. The Gnostics thought (among other things) that the resurrection might just be a spiritual thing, and that Christ was not raised physically, again for similar reasons.

But maintaining any form of Gnostic or Platonic dualism is impossible in life.[5] No-one can sustain such intense 'soul-winning' (leading people to Christ), apart from those with gifts of evangelism, and even they will struggle always to be doing 'spiritual' things. The very people who tend to accuse those of us who enjoy travel of wasting our lives are still whiling away hours at home in their own pursuits.

But not only is it impractical,[6] more importantly it just isn't theological. Apart from a few verses commonly used to justify this belief structure, the grand narrative of the Bible is a very down-to-earth one. Physical things matter. And there's no separating the spiritual from the physical. God's ordinary means of working in the world is to use physical means to do a spiritual work. And we'll see this on our next island-hop, and also in our last chapter where we consider the climax of our home ahead.

*Island*: Espiritu Santo, famous for its white sand and clear waters. Kayak and snorkel with sea-lion puppies and explore the wrecks and reefs
*Location*: My hammock
*Topic*: Travelling with the goal of persuading

At University College, Cork, the free lunch and short talk, 'Hope: light in the darkness', had just ended, and the couple of people not from the Christian Union (mission team) left rapidly. Another attempt at an evangelistic event, another not hugely successful one. But we were determined to keep on trying. Why? Because we were convinced that this was biblical evangelism.

Throughout the book of Acts, you'll find Paul and his mini-mission team travelling to various cities and doing the same thing in most of them.

First, they were always a team sent by the churches – only once do we see Paul firing ahead without others around him, and then he's waiting for them to show up. And Acts 13 shows them being commissioned by the churches, only to return later to report back what God had been doing. For our short-term mission teams and travels, it's a good principle to follow – are we sent by our churches at home? In our Christian Unions we aim to have the backing of our churches back home.

Second, they would usually start in the Jewish synagogue before heading to the marketplace, philosophy halls or places where large numbers of thinkers or people congregated.

Third, they would always persuade, reason, discuss, debate, or do something similar, using proclaimed words of good news.

Much as this helps us as we seek to speak of Jesus on our travels, it will also help us simply to relate well to the culture around us and not be known for being loud-mouthed, culturally insensitive tourists who see only the flaws in the culture they're visiting.

### The unremarkable tourist

We are not given many examples throughout Acts of what this persuading of the people looks like. There's an extensive example relating to a Jewish audience, an extensive one to a more pagan audience and then there are a few smaller inter-changes. So Acts 17:16–34 is really our best effort to consider an audience closely aligned to our own.

Here we see three principles in action:

1. *Identification*: the mission team have clearly done their homework and spent time with people, or in the city. They quote local poets, they've seen local altars, and they know that religiosity is a central tenet of society. As we travel, we'd do well to do similarly, to understand the yearnings and questions in every human heart.
2. *Persuasion*: later, in his letter to the Corinthians, Paul makes the case for his theology of preaching,[7] but here we see his example of persuasion. After seeing where people are at,

he seeks to persuade them of the biblical reality from there. Note that although he confronts them on some things, it's in a far broader context of complimenting them and Identifying with them, as well as pointing out similarities in world views.

3. *Invitation*: this doesn't necessarily mean a call at the end of every meeting for anyone who wants to follow Jesus to come up to the front! But there is a response – some scoff, some to want to hear more, and others accept the good news and join the local fellowship. So, if there is a response, the people must have been invited to do something, in some way.[8]

Paul goes to them (identification), takes their hand (persuasion) and leads them gently a step at a time towards the truth (invitation).[9] Where this happens well on university and college campuses across the UK and Ireland, individuals have come to faith.

*Island*: Malekula, known for its cannibals (now ancient history), rugged mountains and birdwatching. The locals are much friendlier nowadays
*Location*: My hammock
*Topic*: Travelling to support the suffering

Paul's letters are brimming with heart-filled longings and yearnings. And given that some of them are directed at people he's never even met before, it's quite incredible to read. Check out this one to the Colossians:

> We always thank God, the Father of our Lord Jesus Christ,
> when we pray for you, because we have heard of your
> faith in Christ Jesus and of the love you have for all God's
> people . . .
>     For this reason, since the day we heard about you, we
> have not stopped praying for you. We continually ask God
> to fill you with the knowledge of his will.
> (Colossians 1:3–4, 9)

Paul sure wears his heart on his sleeve and follows it through
with action. Perhaps that's how he gets away with some
incredible rebuking and correcting in his letters too. But Paul's
constant longings for his brothers and sisters in Christ (his fellow
Christians) mean that much of his travelling involves suffering
for them, with them and for the gospel's sake (2 Corinthians
11:21–33).

But it's Peter, who was very slow to catch on to Jesus' intended
death and sufferings throughout the Gospels, who brings out a
theology which Paul so clearly agrees with and travels by. In his
first letter he opens with a rhythm of life he expects all who've
been birthed into a living hope to have:

> Suffering now
>     Glory later
> Joy now

The New Testament pattern of church life and mission seems
to care little for comfort or rights. These people have no right
to travel, and nor do we. They have no right to orientate life
around building up comfortable, physical homes, surrounded

by people like them, no right to be in control of their circumstances. Instead, the focus seems to be on doing anything so that all might hear the gospel, and joyfully embracing whatever comes to them in order to allow this to happen. Home is radically different from what we might expect. What a calling!

*Island*: Paama, described by one website as 'paradise on earth', with warm, welcoming people who love their culture and ancestral way of life. At the time of writing they don't have any internet connection – bliss!
*Location*: My hammock
*Topic*: Travelling to the ends of the earth

It's hard to deny the New Testament emphasis that travel essentially echoes the great commissions in their various forms (in each Gospel).[10] From the word 'go', the gospel is moving outwards from Jerusalem to Judea, Samaria and beyond. There's mention of it in every chapter in Acts, either implicitly or explicitly, until in Acts 13:49 and 19:10 we reach the point where all within huge regions are getting the chance to hear and respond to the good news. As the Ethiopian eunuch (Acts 8) takes the good news back to his country, this is perceived as being the ends of the earth at the time.

The 'all nations' that we're called to go to today might be better translated 'all peoples', which is where we get our focus on 'people groups', which we looked at earlier (see note 3 in Chapter 1 for more details).

## Common objections

This emphasis in Acts on travelling to the least-reached peoples with the good news helps us because it answers many common objections today:

- *'Most people could hear the good news if they wanted to.'*
  In which case, most of the struggles of the New Testament seem pointless!
- *'Everyone can go online to find out about Jesus in English / [insert colonial language here].'*
  The internet doesn't exist in certain places, many cultures can't understand colonizing languages, and it's not a biblical model of evangelism to force people to identify with us.
- *'We have great unreached areas on our own doorstep.'*
  Perhaps, but not many of them have no chance at all of hearing of Jesus in their mother tongue in ways they can relate to.
- *'We must build our own church before reaching others.'*
  If this inward-looking attitude had prevailed, would the early Church ever have grown?
- *'Europe is largely under 2 per cent reached. We must first reach here.'*
  If you are in an area that has around 2 per cent following Jesus, then give thanks. At least, let us look at the parts of the world that have no church, no Bible and no Christian community at all.

## Hard truths

You might assume that the above would mean that unengaged (i.e. unreached with the gospel) people groups would win more of our attention as a worldwide Church in terms of future planning. But no. Instead, sadly, few churches have even heard the term 'unengaged', and even fewer prioritize supporting mission to them by praying for more workers. In reality, the pressing needs of our local churches and areas often crowd out this important need.

Millions are going to everlasting death without Christ, and we're sending at least 95 per cent of our money, resources and missionaries to reached places.[11] This is a tragedy that must stop.

My question to everyone is not, 'Are you called to the unengaged world?' but rather, 'The Bible calls the Church to look outwards to all peoples, so what part are you playing?' There are many legitimate reasons why people can't go, but there are many good things that we often choose to put in the way of the best things.

Perhaps the first step could be shaping your travel plans around visiting and supporting workers in unengaged or unreached areas. It sounds trivial that my pleasure travel and sitting on beaches could ever achieve such deep purposes, but such trips and their results have completely changed my outlook on life.

## Takeaways from our island-hopping

It's easy to pick out themes of New Testament travel. Travel is everywhere. But once again we are struggling to find pleasure travel within the types of travel that anyone is seen engaging in.

And do our exotic locations above not jar at times with some of the more serious topics from the New Testament? Does all this mean we shouldn't be travelling for pleasure at all?

The issue isn't really dealt with directly (partly because it wasn't something that the culture of the time was concerned with). It's better considered in the greater light of what we have seen clearly from our travels so far together, and in the context of the missionary purpose above.

As we jump on the boat across the Pacific to Colombia, we'll have plenty of time to consider these things. Sixteen days to be exact, as we sit on board with little Wi-Fi and not much else to consider on this cargo ship. Not quite the long months that it used to take missionaries of old to do this route, though!

**Questions for the road**

- What other types of travel can you think of in the New Testament that we haven't talked about?
- What missionary partnerships do you support? How could you develop those partnerships to a deeper level, both as a church and as an individual?
- Suffering or sacrificial travel is hard to fathom in a pleasure travel industry. What do you think it could look like in reality?
- How can you best identify with those with whom you travel and those you visit?
- What would becoming more intentional about your travels look like?

### Prayer

Generous Father,
just as you sent your Son to this world and
gave of your very self,
so, you send us into this world,
and pray for us with expectant prayers,
that not only would we be one,
but also that those who come to faith
would be one with us,
just as you are one with your Son.
And so, we also ask you to stir in us a great expectancy,
for all you will do in the nations,
as you use weak persuaders like us.
Strengthen us in the midst of suffering to rejoice,
and warm our hearts with your generosity in this world
so much that we overflow with Samaritan joy,
to tell others we meet.
For your glory,
Amen.

**Chapter One** North-west Norway: finding havens of tranquility in the land of the Midnight Sun

**Chapter One** Paris, France: discovering with Sophie that cities are part of God's plan

**Chapter Two** Tunisia: 'beautiful ruins' is a phrase summarizing so much of our travels in a broken yet wonderful world

**Chapter Three** A street market in the Middle East: cultural adventures and lessons in shopping!

**Chapter Four** Cliffs of Moher, Ireland: for me, the feeling of 'home' is found here

**Chapter Six** The Colombian border, shortly after Dan and I had a conversation with a gunman

**CHAPTER SIX**

DYING
TO TRAVEL

Savouring Christ
and finding self

For me to live is Christ, to die is gain.
(The apostle Paul)[1]

A ship in harbor is safe –
but that is not what ships are built for.
(John A. Shedd)[2]

**Destination**: Colombia
**Weather**: Warm, sunny and humid
**Company**: The world cyclist Dan Ross

Dan (my housemate, remember?) and I were back on the road again. In some ways, we were very different. Dan wanted to save every cent possible, whereas I wanted to feel free on holiday without worrying about cost (once we'd budgeted at the start). Dan was also up for more scary challenges and adventures and couldn't understand my lack of enthusiasm for some of his plans.

When on top of a huge towering plateau of rock with crevices that plummeted a hundred feet to the ground, I didn't find it amusing or even tempting to try and jump over the five-foot gap to the other side for the craic. My life was going to be sufficiently in danger at other points in life not to bother this time. So, I sat there, giving him the silent treatment as he laughed and bounded about, jumping over the death-drop not once but as many times as it would amuse him that I was so scared.

But on this trip we were about to encounter a far more scary moment. Welcome to our holiday!

## Alone in rebel territory

I mean, we had been warned that the border is rebel territory where anything goes. But driving through it on a nice summer day seemed so normal. The music was pumping, and it was 6 p.m. already when we managed to pull up at the guard station in the next village, a few miles from the plateau we were going to climb, to register that we were going up this mountain. I did wonder what they would do if we got confronted by rebels up there. We would be miles from this small guard outpost. Even that was assuming that we'd get registered at this hour. After wandering up and down the street a few times to find the guard on duty, we finally registered and set off ... under armed escort!

A fairly hilarious scene. A bright red little car with two lads messing around, a guard truck in front and another armed car behind.

At the road towards the foot of the mountain, one of the cars pulled off and signalled we were to go on. The other followed us. Reaching the closest thing resembling a car park that we ever saw in this part of the world, we parked and got out. The other car wished us well, and suggested we take their local guide to escort us up safely. We looked at each other. Neither of us particularly wanted our hike to be spoiled by a random old man who barely spoke any English and seemed incapable of helping us fight off any rebels who were rumoured to be around. We shrugged – what harm could it be? Easier keeping him than trying to explain that we didn't want him.

And so we headed up. Reaching the top a while later, we explored the kilometre of plateau, put up our tent, kicked a ball around, and then sat down to dinner and sunset.

It was then that we noticed we weren't alone. And it wasn't our guide either, who was now nowhere to be seen. 'I'll see you in the morning' had been his last words about forty minutes before. The only way up the plateau was steep and out of sight, and no approach could have been seen by us. Maybe we'd been too cocky after all.

### Unexpected company

This thought struck us when we saw the athletic build of the man who was walking over the rocks to us, holding a gun. He was in plain clothes. There was nowhere to hide. Thoughts rushed through my head: we were nobodies . . . who would ever want anything to do with us? Just simply two lads having fun travelling.

'Hello!' the voice echoed around the crevices of the plateau, making it feel as though we were surrounded by far more than just this lone gunman. We scrambled to our feet so that we would at least meet this man on a similar level. His calm words of local dialect that followed were not ones that, in my state of panic, I chose to remember from my few language classes I'd had one summer a while ago. Obviously, my face showed that. Phew. The main language now.

After asking us what we were up to, he demanded our passports and asked about the car sitting at the foot of the plateau. I don't know who he thought the car might belong to. 'No, I think bright red little cars must be how local rebels get around these days.' Or at least that's what I might have said if I hadn't been panicking and actually sure that he wasn't himself a rebel. The hire company had obviously thought that giving us the only bright red car in the whole of the country was a fun joke to play, as we hadn't seen one for most of our trip.

It was in these moments that I was grateful that I'd got two passports, at least leaving me with an escape option, should the worst come to the worst. And with British records of colonialism and war, there was no doubt that it was my Irish one that I would be showing.

Bud-ump.
Bud-ump.
Bud-ump.

Our hearts were drums amid an otherwise silent dusk. Did he understand the English on the passports? We didn't care to ask. And the next few words were said with not a smile on his lips.

'Very dangerous. Very, very dangerous up here.'

We hesitated to ask why, unsure of whether the gun butt would move closer to our questioning lips as a reward for our answering back.

## Leave or risk everything

'Very dangerous. You have two choices. You can escape the danger and I will take you down the mountain. Or you can stay up here and risk everything.' Or at least that's what I got from his thick local drawl.

Dan and I glanced at each other. If we were to leave, we at least wanted to know why we were leaving. So, we nervously tried again.

'What is the risk?'
'There are many wild animals here. Wild goats. Wild birds. Wild creatures.'

Well, I didn't know exactly what he said at the end of the list, but I tried hard not to splutter into laughter at the animal list that we were supposedly to be scared of. Wild goats and birds? There wasn't a moving thing in sight! And even so, I doubted if any would merit the 'very dangerous' telling off that we were about to receive. Did I really understand him correctly? Dan clearly hadn't followed. It was my basic language skills that would be the deciding factor as to whether we stayed or went.

We had a stand-off. He still had our passports and clearly wasn't impressed that we didn't respond more to his stern words. He spoke, hoping to add weight to his confrontation.

But we continued to stand. Slowly, giving us our passports back while not taking his eyes off ours, he gave us the kind of look that I'd get from my parents when they clearly disapproved of everything I'd done, but wanted me to learn the hard way.

And as quickly as he'd come, he walked away to leave us alone again with a stunning sunset, miles of untouched landscape and the conviction that I should have paid more attention in school classes. After watching him leave in silence, we whispered: did he really just warn us about wild animals? The doubts were nagging. But we hadn't travelled all this way for nothing. This was stunning. And not to be missed. And besides, the plateau even had a mention in our guidebook (albeit with a caution), so it couldn't be that dangerous!

And so, the craic soon flowed again and the sunset was one of my most memorable ever. Our sleep was much needed, even if nervous. And we awoke to a stunning sunrise, pouring its warmth over the shadow-cast landscape beyond.

### *Our protector arrives*

Our guide appeared out of nowhere, as if by magic, just as we were thinking of leaving. He laughed when we told him about the armed man and our conversation the night before. We laughed with him. Until he declared, 'I laugh because you do not need to worry when I am here. I protected you all night.'

Ah yes . . . of course. An old villager who could barely fight off wild goats was secretly watching over us all night. How very noble. We gave him a suitably generous donation for his 'work' and protection services and made our way back to our bright red rebel vehicle. Happily sitting in the sun, our adventure continued . . . for now.

## The adventure ahead

Situations like that one remind me of the fragility of life and make me question what I'm willing to risk my life for. One of the most famous parkour stars recently died falling from a skyscraper. Several of my sister's friends (all experienced climbers) were climbing in mountains near where they lived. An unexpected snow storm blew in; it was so fierce that they couldn't see their cars, which were only a hundred metres from where they froze to death. Tragic incidents like these remind me of the famous missionary traveller who said: 'Only one life t'will soon be past. Only what's done for God will last.'[3]

Oh no! Here comes the bit in the book when we get told to stop travelling and spend the rest of our days in monastic settlements serving God.

Well, no. But I do think such poignant realizations help us think about some of the biggest themes that are woven throughout the Scriptures. At several points, explicitly, there's a call on an adventure: to die. And by that I don't just mean a physical death, or else there would be no Church left. The death that we're called to die has been described helpfully by my fellow Irishmen in the seventh or eighth century (in what is now referred to as the Cambrai Homily, explained a little by Pope Gregory I and Jerome). Some of these early Celtic Christians were travellers who recorded much of life and spirituality for us. They suggested:

*Red martyrdom*: blood martyrs killed for their faith.
*White martyrdom*: outward ascetics, separating themselves from all society in monasteries or as hermits.
*Green martyrdom*: inward asceticism, like fasting.

To get away from what could be a tendency in some backgrounds to remove oneself from the world, evangelical Christians would often interpret this last one as inward spiritual renewal of *any* variety, which I would argue is closer in balance to the original intention of the verses that inspired these different 'martyrdoms':

> Then Jesus said to his disciples, 'Whoever wants to be my disciple must deny themselves and take up their cross and follow me.'
> (Matthew 16:24)

This verse, and even more the whole swathes of Scripture that follow its theme (as we saw in the last chapter), has continually made the Church uncomfortable with its nice existence in societies that have traditionally been thought of as 'Christian', or in Western cultures with materialistic pleasure on tap.

If your heart is anything like mine, the last thing you want to do with your life is have everything cross-centred, suffering for the sake of Christ and his Church.

I think Francis and Lisa Chan hit the nail on the head when they said: 'Christians have come up with clever ways for why followers of a suffering Servant should look like Kings.'4

And it's largely true in my life. Look at how I spend my time, and what my bank statements say I spend my money on, and you'll have an interesting time seeing what my passions really are. Another way to tell is partly to see what goes on my bucket list as a traveller. What will be the events and travels of the year that you'll wake up for in the morning, or go to sleep dreaming of?

## My bucket list

To answer some of these questions, write down on a piece of paper all the places that you'd love to visit this year. For me, these are just a few:

1. *(The Occupied Territories of) Western Sahara*. I've been to most of the favourite spots in North Africa and love its culture so much that I thought one of the lesser-visited areas would be brilliant to explore.
2. *Vanuatu*. My sister and her newly married husband and their child are living here temporarily before returning to Africa. I'd love to venture out to see more of the paradise islands of the Pacific and my family there, as I so rarely get to spend time with them and I've never seen my niece.
3. *Manchester, England*. I've got close family who are church-planting (leading new fellowships of Christians) in this area, and I'd love to go to support them and see what it is like.

4. *Somewhere within sight of the Northern Lights.* You've already heard my rave about this.
5. *Something spontaneous.* Because too much planning spoils the fun!

After writing the list, I suggest tearing up the paper into small bits and putting it in the recycling bin.

You heard me!

Why? Because our bucket list should not be lord over our year. And if we're letting our calendar be primarily dictated by what it says, then we're letting it be lord, and a rather cruel lord at that. We're worshipping another god by giving it control of the year ahead.

## Asking good questions

To shape a year asking where you can legitimately travel as a Christian is much like asking the question when dating: 'How far can we go and still be Christians?' Or the question on a night out with friends: 'How many drinks are too many?' They just aren't good questions to start with, because they start at the wrong place.

The Creator God, for whom all the nations are as a drop in a bucket, is calling us.

Surely the nations are like a drop in a bucket;
they are regarded as dust on the scales;
he weighs the islands as though they were fine dust.
(Isaiah 40:15)

## Zooming in, panning out

God: the One who made the heights of the Himalayas and the depths of the sea beds. The One who sustains the waves crashing on the shore each hour and each day, by the laws he sets. The One who has created the intricate designs on the butterfly wing, as it flies through the depths of the Grand Canyon.

If we ever grow weary of Instagramming even the small radius of our everyday lives, we have a whole universe to explore. And if the nations really are so small to him, then he'll have even the most powerful of rulers and businessmen quaking and incapable of acting, if he so chooses. For their nations are as a drop in a bucket. Vast oceans of buckets could never even reach the magnitude of God.

So, let's remind ourselves: do we really want to shape this year by exploring that drop at the bottom of a bucket?

Added to that, our bucket list cares nothing for us. In fact, if some circumstance means we get little or nothing on our bucket list ticked off, we'll think it's a rotten year and this will eat us up inside when we see others trotting the globe. But if we do get everything done on our list, then it is no better either. We'll still be eaten inside – as we try to relive those fleeting memories of travel; as we find our heart growing for even bigger and better things in future. Because feeding our bucket list lord will often lead to us sacrificing more to feed it in future. And even if we can control our lusting hearts, what cost will our bucket list lord be to those around us? For with every travel experience, there were other opportunities we did not take to serve others.

## Swapping bucket lists

The danger of all this is that we do what humans are prone to do, and react to the opposite extreme by trying to abandon our bucket list entirely, and instead, without realizing it, create a Christian bucket-list equivalent. For example, I pour so much of my time and energy into thinking about unreached people groups (many in dangerous parts of the world) and how to reach them that it has nearly at times become my ultimate bucket-list goal. This is often the case for travellers who want to make the biggest meaningful impact possible.

In all that, there are some brilliant motives. But I've met many who've given *everything* to go to places where 'red' martyrdom is more likely, only to have their dreams shattered by a long-term illness, being banned from the country, or the death of a family member. Some have realized that, just like letting our bucket lists control our lives, so it is with letting a Christian 'mission-filled' version control us. Those who let their travelling goals be primarily something on this earth, however Christian it may be, soon realize that they've robbed themselves of far greater glories.

And when I start to ask questions of my life stirred by thoughts above, I've found a far more freeing joy in all I do, and a purpose in life. I've discovered that God still delights in letting us explore his world as we seek first his kingdom. Because he's not a stingy God – he just wants what's best for his children. I'll probably still have a bucket list in the back of my head, because I think some of this world is fantastic, but my prayer is that it won't take hold of me. And if that's ever a real struggle, I should keep myself accountable to someone.

## *Living dead*

Not many of us will ever face situations where we'll die physically for our faith (red). Not many of us will be called to vocations or extended times of isolation (white), although I'd recommend trying a day of retreat per holiday with no Wi-Fi, and if you're braver even a silent one. Most of us will live lives of 'green' martyrdom, the third of the options we considered earlier.

It's in this way we are all called to 'live dead',[5] paraphrasing John 12 (and Romans 12:1–2).

> Jesus replied, 'The hour has come for the Son of Man to be glorified. Very truly I tell you, unless a grain of wheat falls to the ground and dies, it remains only a single seed. But if it dies, it produces many seeds. Anyone who loves their life will lose it, while anyone who hates their life in this world will keep it for eternal life. Whoever serves me must follow me; and where I am, my servant also will be. My Father will honour the one who serves me.
>
> 'Now my soul is troubled, and what shall I say? "Father, save me from this hour"? No, it was for this very reason I came to this hour. Father, glorify your name! . . .
>
> 'Now is the time for judgment on this world; now the prince of this world will be driven out. And I, when I am lifted up from the earth, will draw all people to myself.' He said this to show the kind of death he was going to die.
> (John 12:23–28, 31–33)

Glory.

What does glory look like? Or what would the biblical definition of it be? (Please don't look up the dictionary – I'm not sure we're on a wavelength.) Perhaps a film soundtrack would be easier to put to it.

It's a big theme throughout the Scriptures – that God is the all-glorious One who deserves all glory to be given back to him. In fact, one of the prophets goes further, to suggest that he is so glorious that his awesome glory can't be shared with another (Isaiah 42:8). Like the all-consuming fireball that is our sun. When things get too close and casual – boom! Gone. It's not arrogant of the sun; it's just reality. That's the very heart of what it is to be the sun. And so, magnified by millions, and in a very personal, loving community, it is with God.

## Shared glory

But what we see in this passage, and others, is that those who follow Jesus are with him in his presence. And the presence of the Son of Man (in Daniel 7) is that of the Ancient of Days (God the Father). This long problem of the world is coming to an end. The separation between a holy God and his sinful people is over. One has come who can lead us into his presence, through his death, drawing people to himself. The great glory of the ever-lasting God will be no problem to us, because, amazingly, we'll be united with him, basking in his glory, his presence, his character, never to be separated, regardless of whether or not we have doubts and even if we struggle in this world.

## Shared suffering

Sometimes we wonder whether following Jesus is ever worth it. Sometimes we'd rather have everything this world is offering. That relationship with someone who isn't a passionate Jesus follower whom we meet on our travels. The willingness to sit back and not speak up when situations of injustice arise for others on our travels. The right to spend our free time and money as we jolly well wish. The nice church down the road that doesn't want us to commit for years to the hard work, and doesn't mind much if we're away all the time.

### Shared eternal life

But Jesus sits with us in our struggles. He is the ultimate grain of wheat that falls into the ground and dies. Without this, there would be no fruit – it would just have been a very good life lived. But with him, there is everything – many seeds! Seed that multiplies and explodes into maximum life with the Son, united to him without doubt.

We follow in his footsteps, dying to self in his strength, in order to have life to the full. When we get to see Christ's glory and share in it, we all become martyrs. Our dying changes from dying to travel to dying to self. But just like those seeds, in dying to self we'll find ourselves and find new life in his name.

## *Truly free: giving up everything, receiving even more*

For me, there's a dilemma. I'm sorely tempted by all the travel options. So much so that I find myself away from my home church more than I would like. Yet, the more I find myself committing to the church community, the more I feel free. Free to be who I am, free not to have to produce evangelistic results myself, free to be weak in front of others (they see everything), free to fail, free to ask for forgiveness, free to keep short accounts with people I see lots. Free!

Being away from home and church as we go travelling a lot robs us of the above. We're unable to live in such a unique community:

unable to contribute, unable to benefit. We're unable to love one another deeply and effectively.

> 'By this everyone will know that you are my disciples, if you love one another.'
> (John 13:35)

God has revealed his means of working in this world: his Church, presiding over his word and the Lord's Supper, and guarding them by healthy church discipline. If I choose to travel on weekends and deliberately forsake my local church gathering – the people of God whom I've committed myself to – then I neglect him. And, tragically, I start to reject him.

I sit here always so tempted to book that next flight. And all for good reason. 'What about those friends I haven't seen in so long who even support me in my work, whom I could visit?' 'What about my family some miles away whom I am called to love?' 'What about that other church, which wants me to share reports about my work?' 'Will one more Sunday away really be a problem?' I think to myself.

So, this semester, in order to keep me home-based, I'm asking my community group to keep me accountable, thereby keeping me from thinking I can waltz off on my travels and it won't affect anyone. Yes, I can think it will have no effect on my spirituality, but I'd be wrong. There's so much more freedom and joy in community as God meant it to be.

It's hard to express how rewarding such a lifestyle really is, committing to loving God first and loving our neighbour as ourselves, unless we've actually experienced it. In an individualized world, it can even appear today that what was the norm for Christians back in the early Church, being in local community, is an add-on. But as we move on to consider the future of travel in the years to come, we'd do well first to adapt to the changes of the past.

**Questions for the road**

- We were designed to share in life together as a church community. How can we go about this better practically?
- What might practising this while we're on the road look like?
- Are there things that you need to discuss with more mature Christians? Why not stop, make a note of them or ask someone now?

### Prayer

Beautiful One,
we bathe at the fountain of your goodness.
We revel in the shared love between you and your Son.
We bask in the glory that you have always said would not
be shared with another.
Yet we are aware that, as we do this, we die to self.
We thank you that the ultimate seed has gone into the
ground and died already, that we might find life.
But we pray you would lead us in his footsteps,
empower us by your Spirit,
lead us into new depths of dying,
that life may be all the richer.
For you alone are worth it.
Amen.

### CHAPTER SEVEN

### MADE FOR
### BETTER TRAVEL

A new way
of travelling

There are far better things ahead
than any we leave behind.
(C. S. Lewis)[1]

Real development is not leaving things behind,
as on a road, but drawing life from them, as from a root.
(G. K. Chesterton)[2]

*Destination*: To infinity – and beyond!
*Weather*: Vacuum
*Company*: Another race?

We had been hiking for several hours, zig-zagging up the steep slopes of the mountain to one of Ireland's tallest summits. Every few minutes the young, high-pitched voice behind me, mounted on two tiny, weary legs, would ask: 'Are we nearly there yet?'

To which I probably didn't give very wise answers. Every mound that I thought was us nearing the top of the mountain was actually only another blind summit, appearing to be the last one before the top, but never becoming this reality. And blind it was in more than one way: as the mist had descended on Mount Brandon, for miles around nothing could be seen apart from the short distance ahead. Was it all going to be for nothing?

But when we got there, it was worth it. Like a film scene, perfectly rolling in without final steps towards the summit, the clouds had decided to behave for us, and for the first time we saw the full ridge stretching out beneath us, and the peninsulas stretching all the way down the Irish coast into the Atlantic Ocean for miles around. A panorama that even I, who am frequently up Irish mountains, rarely catch a glimpse of. The depth and colour were such that they couldn't be caught on any picture I might try to take, so I just stood there in awe.

Looking back down the path we had come up, it all seemed so clear. All the many humps we'd laboured over, wondering whether each was the last one. It was all worth it now, without a shadow of a doubt.

## *Looking back*

And that's where I hope we've reached in seeing God's panorama of travel. Sometimes it can be so very hard to see where the path is going when we're in the middle. But standing looking back, with the full picture, it all makes sense. This will be what will make the new heaven and new earth all the more spectacular, because we'll be able to see back through history without our limited lenses. Yes, we'll still be very much us, and perhaps even us with lenses. But those lenses will no longer colour our vision in negative ways that used to cloud our vision of God, other people and our world. For the first time, our perspective on travel will be pure.

Looking back is always easy, though, even at the current point of our lives. There are always doomsayers in every field. And sure enough, as the travel industry took off, in 1946 the famous words of one travel writer were about to be recorded: 'I do not expect to see many travel books in the near future.'[3]

How wrong he was! It happened, and then it multiplied a hundred times over, as people visited the same spots with different lenses, and at different times of year, and reported on them in different ways. And still, with thousands of similar sites and hours of videos online, and much more, no-one is seeing the end of the travel industry yet. It will morph and change, as environmental policies change, as sustainable tourism develops, and with shifting world events – but it is not likely to go anywhere fast.

## The future of travel

I can say this as confidently as anyone who is trying to look forward can, partly because of where the philosophy under-girding this travel craze has come from. You see, we've hit the arrivals lounge after several hundred years of philosophy. We may like to think of ourselves as incredible travellers, but we're also a product of our age. In a nutshell, the Enlightenment dawned in the late seventeenth century, and reason and rationality were exalted above all. Jumping on from that, post-modernism hit, as a response to the reason-dominating, truth-orientated world view of the past. 'Can we know anything?'

and 'What even is truth?' were the questions that left us with nothing to unite around.

No longer was there a truth-system that connected communities and formed the fabric of society, like the old Judeo-Christian way of life might have done in some places before. But when truth is abandoned from the public square and from discussion, something must fill the vacuum that follows. And that something became (individual) experience.

Experience was the trump card that topped all others. As well as changing public-square discourse, so that it became more about what people felt and experienced, we also had a technology boom that allowed cheap air travel and connection over the internet, to name just a few things that combined and paved the way for us, an experiential and international generation that values travel so highly.

## Throwback time?

As usual, voices concerned with the negative impacts of such trends of individualism were speaking out against the fads. And we've already noted some of those very real impacts and trends as we've considered the fallenness of travel. But what can be done about it? The cries were to turn back the years to the 'good old days' when we weren't addicted to such things, when there was more social fabric to society for communities to unite around, and when travel was a luxury.

But to turn back time is not only currently impossible physically, but impossible philosophically and technologically. Are we to undo what we know about the technology and inventions that gave us air travel? Are we to take away those aspects of the internet that gave us dreams and made the world smaller? Are we to reverse beyond the point in philosophical thought where everything came undone and we became obsessed with individualized pleasure?

So many thousands upon millions of small decisions, small advances, tiny changes have happened in all of these fields to lead us to where we are today in this overarching narrative. Even if we thought those decades of childhood were the good old days where everything was rosy (for which I think you'd be hard pressed to make a convincing case, in any generation), still it would be impossible to return there. The road once travelled cannot be traversed again in reverse. We cannot turn back time.

The only thing that would happen if people and communities tried to reverse time is that they would end up in an isolated subsection of a world that continues to advance and move onwards, playing no role whatsoever and convincing few others ever to join.

So, for travel pessimists, it all appears as if it's doom and gloom. But for us who travel, what is the future? Well, if going back is not possible, the only thing we're left with is some version of going forward. And the one thing we'll continue to have is what we've seen of God's panorama as we've considered it throughout Scripture.

## *Beautiful ruins restored*

Here's a panorama where Christians recognize both the beauty and the ruin of the world that lies in front of them, delighting in the former and seeking to restore the latter by steering the direction in which travel is going, by being involved positively in the latest developments and advances in technology, psychology, science and art, in so far as a Christ-exalting life will allow that to happen.

This is why I named my blog 'aljabr' (the Arabic from which we get the English word algebra), which means restoration or the uniting of broken parts – far more exciting than algebra for most of us! I look forward to a day when travel in the new heaven and the new earth will not have any of the pitfalls we've encountered. When aspects of our culture, world and life, which we thought were fleeting or had long disappeared, come back to even fuller levels. Ultimately, we can only restore things within our small capabilities given to us by the great Restorer, One who will restore everything to levels even better than those of the Garden of Eden.[4]

What this restoration looks like in the meantime will be different in every field of academia and culture. To be sure, trying to achieve a 'Christian culture' should not be our goal, so that we can feel comfortable in society. Our goals should primarily be Jesus' goals for the world. And that might look like being a minority, learning how to engage positively and share good news in a world that is rebelling against Jesus. The quicker we learn not to try and hold on to the perceived 'Christendom'[5] of the past in our lands, the more we'll be able to devote time and energy to shaping the road to come, by being salt and light in every area of the world, including travel.

## *Looking into the future*

What would this look like in the future of the travelling world? One of the exciting ventures of the travel industry is the possibility of radical travel unlike any other before. Elon Musk and others have inspired a generation of dreamers and inventors, willing to take risks and think of outrageous ideas, like the Hyperloop that will take pods in vacuum tunnels from places like New York to Sydney in a matter of an hour or two, with no delays because of weather or other vehicles! The world would get one size smaller again. What was a journey of six months on a ship many years ago, and is now a day's travel by plane, could become a matter of one episode of a TV show away. Incredible!

Instead of seeing only the pitfalls, could we see the potential for closer family ties across borders, more cross-cultural understanding, and the end of a certain level of poverty as food and supplies can be transported quicker and much more easily? Could Christians be the forerunners in putting forward models for developing real, diverse community in such a world?

On top of that, the space race is on, to get space tourism up and going. Could people conceivably visit places like the Moon or even consider living in habitable locations further down the line? Travel is not going away soon (pardon the pun), but it will reinvent itself. There's something about an inquisitive humanity that is inspiring. There's something about our universe that gives us many unknowns still to explore. Could there be something else out there we haven't yet discovered? Could Christians discover something that would even further increase our confidence in our Creator God?

## *Enjoying now*

As we drive onwards with the next advance and push towards new, bigger and better things, we must be careful to live in the moment and enjoy each step, rather than functionally chase after the next thing and miss the journey as part of the experience. Which is easier said than done, as any traveller will know.

> A good traveller has no fixed plans, and is not intent on arriving.
> (Lao Tzu[6])

## *Behind the glossy brochure*

Just consider the amount of time spent on administration for the average travel trip and you'll be well aware how hard it is just to live in the moment! It can be easy to think that being intentional about everything in life would be exhausting. But if you love something, it only feels partially like effort. Most things flow from our heart's love or our world view, and the rest takes hard work to cultivate. Even living in the moment will be hard if you do not love it.

So, people ask me, is always having a secondary (or primary) purpose in your travelling not exhausting and robbing you of the very fact you're enjoying travelling? Quite honestly, for the most part, the answer is 'no'. If it's my love (loving God, loving others), then this travelling will come increasingly naturally to me as I journey on in my Christian faith.

And for the moments when this is not the case? Well, it's chores now for 'jam tomorrow'! And don't think for a moment that hedonistic, secular travel is any less of a chore or more rewarding.

The glossy travel brochure paints a false reality. The three-minute internet video doesn't show you the hours of bookings, cancellations, tensions in relationships, sicknesses, rainy days and mishaps, not to mention the hours perfecting video footage to make it all seem amazing.

## Coming home, feeling free

Intentionality *can* be exhausting, but being intentional for Jesus is being intentional for a Master whose 'yoke is easy' and whose 'burden is light', One who desires us to enjoy the 'rest' of a homecoming. Imagine the feeling of safety and comfort: the buzz as your Wi-Fi connects to your home network, and messages from friends and family come in; the smell of coffee; the warm embrace of a housemate. This is what coming home is.

But this coming home can also be a finding of yourself and who you were created to be. And it can be done on the road, far away from physical home, while you're living for the moment. Or it can be done in the regular humdrum rhythms of normal working life, getting up from the same bed as you always do, going downstairs to the same situation that always greets you. It's a coming home to your Maker, and a realizing that it is only living with him that will make life fully freeing.

## Finding home

It's 8 a.m. and I'm currently sitting in the Glendalough International Hostel in the Wicklow Mountains in Ireland. I'm staying here as a cheap night away from travelling around Ireland with work, but also because I've heard that some of the trail runs at the top of the hills round the lakes are stunning. Little did I know that I'd be out running at 5 a.m., and arrive back in at 7 a.m. to find my room-mates still sleeping. They probably thought such a tranquil hostel didn't have these late-night partygoers and early morning flight-seekers that so often ruin the hostel night's sleep.

But getting up for 5 a.m. runs doesn't really feel like who I am. There are 'runners' who do that every day or regularly, like my fellow runner. But I'm definitely not one of them.

But who am I? What's my identity?

I have many friends and I meet people all the time on their travels who are trying to find this out. Generally, you can tell either from what they post on social media, or from where they invest their time, money and life. Particularly among those who travel, such questions are huge, because traditional ties to family or nationality are so often rejected (though in some cases nationality becomes a big outward identity, even if the person is in crisis and no longer feels like that inwardly when they're back home). The traveller, to some extent, will have to journey alone in finding their identity, as so often their experiences will be unique.

And perhaps that has to be key: *we are unique*. Perhaps not as unique as we'd like to think in our shared humanity, but unique nonetheless. We have to be more than the sum of our parts, and we desperately hope that is true. As humans we are sexual beings, but we're *more than* our sexuality, important as it is. As humans we're connected beings, but we're *more than* our connections and relationships. And as humans we're creative beings in our jobs, hobbies and elsewhere, but we're *more than just* 'a painter' or 'a football player'.

And the trouble with all of these things is that if we let them define us, we'll be ruined. We'll sell ourselves short of who we really are or, even worse, end up mentally unstable. And yet, that's what we constantly do in a bid to make ourselves seem something.

So, what's the solution? Invest our identity in so many things that even if they go wrong we'll still have a well-balanced life? Risky, but it normally pays off, unless you suffer some catastrophe. That's largely the secular response (with variations on a theme).

Or, what if we could have an identity beyond ourselves? Many would immediately think that this is demeaning – a denial of our uniqueness and everything that we are. And what would it even look like? Most world views that promise this end up being nonsense claims, because that religion or world view just becomes part of an inner struggle to achieve. If you do badly at the world view or religion, you're back down doubting your identity, or struggling mentally. It's just one more part of life.

But it was being shown an identity outside myself that freed me truly to start to get to know myself over time. An identity that had nothing to do with my performance in life or whether or not something was removed from me.

And that identity was, as you'll know by now, Jesus and being found in him. Not in my performance of following him, or my religiosity. But in him, himself. And I've found that because he claims to have made everything (including me), through God the Father, and therefore knows me better than I know myself, I can find myself more and more, as I delve deeper into knowing and experiencing my identity in him.

This means:

- I can face serious sports injuries without fearing my identity will be taken away;
- I can sit beside Republican and Loyalist alike in my home city, and chat to both and concede some things to both politically, because my identity is not in my politics (even if I am still passionate about it);
- I was able to face being given the diagnosis of a long-term medical condition that would shape my life, largely because my identity is not in my health or working capabilities;
- I can face and even enjoy singleness (without porn, sex or even masturbation) because, much as I am a sexual being, I am not defined by it. I am freed to enjoy sex as my Creator intended it;
- I can face the times when I severely doubt the evidence for Jesus, because ultimately the truth (or lack of) doesn't rely on *my* reasoning alone, but on things outside myself (which, I can say, give us good grounds for belief).

My identity is in him, as a 'loved child of God', one who is destined for a better world to come.

And that's freeing!

I'm free to stop travelling the world (metaphorically and physically) in order to find myself (and now just to do it to enjoy him and his world). I'm free to try to better love others who are radically different to me, because if my identity is secure in Jesus Christ I need not fear anything else and can focus all my time and energy on looking outwards, even when people are hard to love.

So, fellow traveller, let's not allow 'Christian' or 'Jesus' just to become another word on our list of identities. Let's lose ourselves in him! And truly find ourselves again in him.

## Heavenly minded, but still of earthly use?

If you find your identity in someone like Jesus, though, won't that absorb a lot of time that could be better used in this world to act wisely, enjoy life and serve others? Most of us may quake when we want to mix God and anything! For many of us in Ireland, he is the ultimate show-stopper, the straitjacket that has bored us for one Mass too many, and robbed us of the pleasure of going out and enjoying life. He is the guilt stick in the corner, raised to hit us over the knuckles, should we enjoy ourselves a bit too much. And surely, travelling the world is probably in that category – most good things seem to be! We think God is a bit like Father Ted with a 'down with this sort of thing' sign, out to curb our freedom, for no particular reason.

Contrary to all that, C. S. Lewis says some fascinating things:

> It would seem that Our Lord finds our desires not too strong,
> but too weak. We are half-hearted creatures, fooling about with
> drink and sex and ambition when infinite joy is offered us, like
> an ignorant child who wants to go on making mud pies in a slum
> because he cannot imagine what is meant by the offer of a holiday
> at the sea. We are far too easily pleased.[7]

C. S. Lewis would suggest that the cry of God when we spend our lives craving the next travel experience, lusting over the holiday photos that our best friend just put up online, living for our holidays, or some more subtle versions of the above, is that we are too easily pleased. We're like the child in the slum. Ironically, the holiday at the sea is nowhere to be found in our lives. Lewis seems to be saying that God would urge: 'Dream bigger! There's far more out there.'

And not more holiday, or more world either. But more of the infinite One who made it all! If travel is *so* good, then how much more the One who generously gave it all so freely.

All very nice, but how do we know this 'God' is not just a projection of our imagination, a comfort blanket for weak people, or simply wish-fulfilment? Where are the signs that should be so obvious and just where we want them to be? (Huge subject, small book!) Lewis continues:

The Christian says, 'Creatures are not born with desires unless satisfaction for those desires exists. A baby feels hunger: well, there is such a thing as food. A duckling wants to swim: well, there is such a thing as water. Men feel sexual desire: well, there is such a thing as sex. If I find in myself a desire which no experience in this world can satisfy, the most probable explanation is that I was made for another world. If none of my earthly pleasures satisfy it, that does not prove that the universe is a fraud. Probably earthly pleasures were never meant to satisfy it, but only to arouse it, to suggest the real thing. If that is so, I must take care, on the one hand, never to despise, or to be unthankful for, these earthly blessings, and on the other, never to mistake them for the something else of which they are only a kind of copy, or echo, or mirage. I must keep alive in myself the desire for my true country, which I shall not find till after death; I must never let it get snowed under or turned aside; I must make it the main object of life to press on to that country and to help others to do the same.[8]

The French existentialist Camus said, from a secular perspective: 'It is necessary to obtain substitutes for immortality. Because I desired eternal life, I slept with whores and drank for whole nights on end.'[9]

You see, we *were* made for another world, a better world.

A new heaven and earth where the infinite God will whisper, 'Bigger, bigger! Dream bigger!', and we'll wish we had never spent so long in slums, playing with mud pies without him.

Finding ourselves in Christ, and then finding out more about ourselves through that lens, we start making sense of the new heaven and new earth, which will be centred on the worship of Christ. We'll grow more eternally in the depth of our worship and being, starting now imperfectly, and rolling on into an eternal exploration to come. That's something our materialistic age doesn't necessarily get, as a paradise with a person at the centre of it is not perceived to be good news to someone whose aim is stuff.

What does this mean for a worshipping future to come in paradise? Revelation 21 answers our questions well:

> Then I saw 'a new heaven and a new earth,' for the first heaven and the first earth had passed away, and there was no longer any sea. I saw the Holy City, the new Jerusalem, coming down out of heaven from God, prepared as a bride beautifully dressed for her husband. And I heard a loud voice from the throne saying, 'Look! God's dwelling-place is now among the people, and he will dwell with them. They will be his people, and God himself will be with them and be their God. "He will wipe every tear from their eyes.

There will be no more death" or mourning or crying or pain,
for the old order of things has passed away.'...

I did not see a temple in the city, because the Lord God
Almighty and the Lamb are its temple. The city does not need the
sun or the moon to shine on it, for the glory of God gives it light,
and the Lamb is its lamp. The nations will walk by its light, and the
kings of the earth will bring their splendour into it. On no day will
its gates ever be shut, for there will be no night there. The glory
and honour of the nations will be brought into it. Nothing impure
will ever enter it, nor will anyone who does what is shameful or
deceitful, but only those whose names are written in the Lamb's
book of life.
(Revelation 21:1–4, 22–27)

Here we have the fulfilment of history. A perfected new heaven
and new earth that we can finally feel at home in, because it's
where we were made to be – back in a restored relationship with
our Maker, under his goodness, in a restored city and land that
will never again suffer a curse or be broken. God's people from
all nations are united in God's paradise, around God himself.

It's good news for the traveller, not just because of the new
heaven and earth to explore but more because of the Creator at
the heart of it.

The response of a Jesus follower to travel is not primarily that
of Homer's Odysseus,[10] who was trying to sail past the most
powerful, alluring songs of the Greek Sirens on the rocks nearby
(the fate of many a sailor), by putting beeswax in his crew's ears
and binding himself to the mast so they couldn't be lured. The
binding and beeswax does indeed work for him, but I'm not sure
it necessarily does so in real life when our hearts are captivated.

No, when my heart yearns to explore this world and to travel, or spends its unproductive hours mulling over what already was, I need a better song to be sung. A more alluring one. One that is so sweet, so clear, so all-consuming that all other songs sound a faint and distant clanging in comparison.

And so, back to my time in Morocco, lying on a beach in the sun with Annabel, Brian and Jo, I wonder what I would say to that question we asked right at the start. How can we make the most of our travels – the missionary, the NHS workers from overseas or me, a random Irish chap working with Christian students?

I hope we've grown in our understanding of who God is, what his heart for this world is, how we can all continue to walk this path together, as we explore more of what he has for us, in the places he has called us to, and as we listen to his sweet, clear and all-consuming song together.

It's the song of our Maker, One who knows that I am made for something more. It woos me to taste sweeter joys and be deeply satisfied in a broken, suffering world.

### Questions for the road

- As you think about where society is headed, are you inclined towards optimism or pessimism?
- Do you meditate upon the eternal future? Why/why not? How could you start doing this more? What excites you about this as a traveller?

- Where do you find your identity? Where do other people think your identity lies?
- What has struck you most from reading this short springboard on faith and travel? Why not check out the resource list and recommended reading at the back for ways you can keep thinking about this topic?

---

**A traveller's prayer**

Lord Jesus,
what an adventure it is knowing you,
following you and being led by you!
We're privileged to be called to embark on this journey;
we're thankful that you have been by our side
every step of the way.
And when unknowns face us, we're grateful for
what lies ahead that we can be certain about:
a new heaven and a new earth;
a future with a travelling God at the heart of it;
an eternity to explore the depths of your being and
revel in the infinite oceans of your love, where we
can dive into the cool, refreshing waters and swim
without finding either bottom or end.
Help us as we meditate upon your goodness and
seek to live for you with our whole heart and being,
as we yearn for that day when you appear again.
Amen.

---

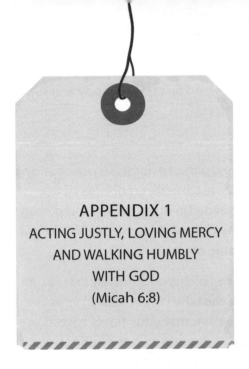

## APPENDIX 1
### ACTING JUSTLY, LOVING MERCY AND WALKING HUMBLY WITH GOD
#### (Micah 6:8)

When you're on holiday, you just want to relax, right? I know that the last thing that I want on my mind is responsibility. Give me a beach, an outdoor adventure or any place where I don't have to think.

And that's why it's hard for the Christian, because our holidays shouldn't leave God behind.

### Ethical questions as we go

Thinking through the following questions before you travel, or before you reach your destination, should help you, but many of them are so big that we could easily have written whole chapters on them (you'll find more at <https://aljabr7.wordpress.com/book/>). You might like to come back to these questions once you return from your travels, or even before you leave next time.

Why not grab a friend or a travel buddy and see what you make of them together?

**Money**

*Scenario 1: Giving gifts to a homeless person in a poverty-stricken South African township while on holiday.*
Is your giving needed in order to help this person survive, or will it prolong a mindset of dependency, when this person could earn a living some other way?

*Scenario 2: Overspending on a holiday that you thought would be cheap, but hidden costs kept creeping in.*
How can you ensure that your travel costs don't spiral beyond your budget? Did you make a basic budget to start with? Do you allow for generosity to others when setting it? What about a percentage for unexpected costs?

*Scenario 3: Ensuring that the cheapest-priced item or holiday isn't that way because people are suffering or short-changed to make it possible for you.*
Do you know where your goods and services come from, or are you simply going on what is most convenient? Is it OK to try and make up for any dodgy decisions by giving retrospectively to charities that help similar disadvantaged people? For example, if you are buying an item of clothing made by a local person who might not be paid much, is it OK to support a charity that fights for better pay for such workers?

*Scenario 4: Going to a country that has just been struck by a terror attack and whose economy is in dire trouble as a result.*
Should we gather round and support countries that have suffered unjustly (if the risk to the traveller is legitimately not a high

one)? Alternatively, are we encouraging an unhealthy dominance of an unstable tourism-based economy by doing so?

**Scenario 5:** *Giving a tip to the 'parking attendant' in Naples, Italy, who stood by your car to protect it while you were away.*
So much unemployment among disabled and less fortunate members of society in certain cultures is caused by gangs. By giving to this man, are you supporting and promoting the culture of gangs? Or are you just helping a man who needs your support?

**Scenario 6:** *Painting an orphanage in Cambodia.*
Is this something that could take jobs away from sustainable local businesses? Or is the experience of helping a number of (often Western) people to see inside a different culture as they do this worth the cost to the local business?

## Photography

**Scenario 7:** *Taking a photo of someone in a Vietnam street because they looked like the quintessentially Vietnamese person.*
When does enjoying a country turn into exploitation? Would you be happy if tourists took your picture without asking? What might be the difference between the two?

## Environment

**Scenario 8:** *Flying to all of our destinations.*
We all know that flying affects the environment. Have you investigated the data that links our carbon footprint to the effects we are seeing in climate change? Or do you just excuse your travelling by saying it is not very much? How could you travel using fewer flights? Have you considered using carbon off-setting?

**Scenario 9**: *Creating lots of plastic waste as you travel in Tunisia, where recycling in rural areas is little practised.*

How can you cut down on throwing away waste while you travel? Could you plan ahead and save your recyclable items for those cities that have recycling services? Why not buy less to start with, or carry spare cloth bags to use instead of plastic ones?

## Culture

**Scenario 10**: *Going to central Asia (Tajikistan) and being presented with a menu that you don't understand, by a local person who doesn't speak much English.*

How can you show a willingness to learn even a few words in the local language, rather than expecting everyone to learn yours? Could you push the boat out and try new foods or cultural practices? How can you honour others and see the best of their culture without letting the negatives affect your whole mindset? Why not keep a record of things you are thankful for, as you travel?

These are just a few selected questions with scenarios that you might encounter when you travel, but there are many, many more. Why not send me your burning ethical questions?

## APPENDIX 2
### TEN TRAVEL TIPS

In no particular order, here are some top tips for your travels abroad.

1. *Find out what God is doing locally.* Why not spend time planning what church you'll visit locally, even if it uses a different language? This will still be an encouragement to others, and to you too in small ways. Or in places with fewer churches, why not ask around to see if there is a local missionary whom you could meet and encourage? Often this person will be willing to give you local insights that you would never otherwise have received.

2. *Be part of what God is doing locally.* Even on holiday it doesn't take much energy to start the day with an expectant heart, praying that God would open our eyes to someone who might be spiritually hungry or someone

whom we can help. And why not then think twice about constantly wearing headphones as you travel? Consider carrying a Gospel to give away or a multi-lingual Bible-resource app that you can point others to.

3. *Remember, for the packing list:*

   (a) a photocopy of your passport (in case the real thing gets lost/stolen), or a picture of it emailed to yourself
   (b) basic medication, painkillers or first aid (harder to find in most places, particularly if a foreign language is involved)
   (c) a second form of payment (for when your bank doesn't realize you're abroad and blocks your card or similar)
   (d) a plug converter or adaptor for the destination country
   (e) spare underwear and a toothbrush in your hand luggage (because your suitcase or bag won't always arrive immediately, alas)
   (f) a keep-cup or water bottle that you can refill anywhere (to save on waste and to keep you hydrated as you travel)
   (g) a battery pack to recharge your mobile or other devices in emergencies (more common to buy now than previously)
   (h) a small padlock with key for bags or hostel cupboards, and a money belt/strap for under your clothes (being discerning without being cynical is wise).

4. *Blend in with the locals.* Why not look up what types of clothing are acceptable, what local festivals are on, and what interaction with the opposite sex is appropriate? Some of my best times away have been during cultural festivals, but travelling during certain seasons can be harder (e.g. Ramadan in a Muslim country) or more

expensive (if everyone is there all at once). Discover when it is customary for local shops to shut and open.

5. *Beat the weather, and don't let it beat you.* If you are struggling to sleep at night in a hot country, why not try laying a wet cloth over your chest and pouring water on it whenever you wake up hot again? It may not be air conditioning as such, but it should help you sleep. Equally, remembering sun cream, insect repellent, a hat, appropriate layers of clothing and good footwear can make all the difference between an exhausting holiday and an enjoyable one.

   I had a Taiwanese friend who came to explore Ireland for one month, and he rented a room in my house as his base. After one week of him sitting inside, I asked him why he was not outside enjoying Ireland? 'I am waiting for it to stop raining,' he said! The next day I gave him my coat, and we went out in the rain together. We can't wait for the perfect weather or expect the travel-brochure sunset every day in order to be happy.

6. *Ask good questions.* If you want to grow and learn about a culture, why not find your way off the beaten track to places where tourists don't go so much? Perhaps even getting intentionally 'lost' somewhere in order to explore unknowns? It can be daunting to be vulnerable and admit not knowing something, but asking questions of locals can be richly rewarding.

   Before you criticize something in another culture, why not ask a local for a perspective on it, or try and think of a positive aspect of this culture for which you can show appreciation? Or, if language is a problem, why not read about the culture as you travel, in a history book, a novel or a travel guide? This brings a place to life and explains so much.

7. *Some phone apps to help you travel*

   (a) CityMapper (for transport in major cities worldwide)
   (b) Maps.me (for some maps that you can download, which will save you data)
   (c) YouVersion (to save the weight of a large Bible)
   (d) Your airline's app (to save printing boarding passes)
   (e) A tourism app (like TripAdvisor, that gives local reviews)

8. *Enjoy the moment.* It's a bit of a cliché, but you'll only experience this moment once. If you're so busy taking a hundred photos (which you may not look back on more than once), or rushing on to the next thing, you'll fail to have full enjoyment of the things around you.

9. *Know how to cut costs*

   - Search for flights in an 'incognito' internet browser.
   - Eat away from tourist areas.
   - Explore currency rates before you go and estimate what you might need (to cut down on multiple transaction costs).
   - Schedule a trip round cheap flights rather than deciding where to go and then seeing what flights are available.
   - Cut aeroplane hold luggage and buy some things cheaper on arrival.
   - Realize that some costs are hidden costs: yes, that flight may have been only twenty euros, but getting to the airport by taxi at 6 a.m. to catch it may double that cost.

- If you're part of a group, work out what budget each of you has, so that you all have similar expectations and know what each person wants to spend money on.

10. *Never forget what it is to be a foreigner.* Life soon returns to normal again back home, and the rush of normal life means we often forget to see our world through fresh eyes, or to notice tourists like us, who are walking around and would love to meet a local. Why not intentionally leave space for interacting with such people or hosting people in your home through something like CouchSurfing?

I'm sure there are plenty of other great tips that I have missed, so why not get in touch with your suggestions, and I'll include the best ones on my blog?

Happy travelling!

# NOTES

### Introduction: #wanderlust

1. Louis Charles Fougeret de Monbron, *Le Cosmopolite ou Le Citoyen Du Monde* (MHRA Critical Texts, 1750) (translation mine).
2. Marcel Proust, *The Remembrance of Things Past* (Penguin, 1913) (translated C. K. Moncrieff).
3. 'A people group is an ethno-linguistic group with a common self-identity that is shared by the various members. For strategic purposes it is the largest group within which the gospel can spread without encountering barriers of understanding or acceptance. There are 11,741 people groups in the world. A people group is considered unreached (UPG) when there is no indigenous community of believing Christians able to engage this people group with church planting. Technically speaking, the percentage of evangelical Christians in this people group is less than 2 per cent. The groups that I refer to here are often referred to as "Unengaged Unreached people groups" (UUPG). They are unengaged when there is no church planting strategy, consistent with evangelical faith and practice, underway. Gathering believers and planting churches are the keys to establishing an effective and multiplying presence among these people groups. 3,178 of these people groups are in this condition, consisting of 220 million people.' Excerpts taken from <www.peoplegroups.org>.

4. A terrorist group often linked to Islam.
5. The Islamic time of fasting during daylight hours for approximately forty days. Given that it often falls around the summer solstice, this is very tough, as many continue working.

## 1. In the land of the Midnight Sun

1. J. R. R. Tolkien, *The Lord of the Rings: Part One, The Fellowship of the Ring* (Boston, MA: Houghton Mifflin, 1987).
2. Sometimes we can get caught up in the science of Genesis 1 – 3 or the language of 'subduing' and miss the incredible things the author wants us to know. But for those of you who still have questions about the more controversial elements of creation, check out the recommended reading for other places to explore.
3. *Five Minutes with: Professor Brian Cox*, aired on the BBC on <http://news.bbc.co.uk/2/hi/sci/tech/8522608.stm> (last accessed February 2018).

## 2. Travelling east of Eden

1. *Mr. Nobody*, directed by Jaco Vam Dormael (2009). Trailer: <www.imdb.com/title/tt0485947/videoplayer/vi23832857?ref_=tt_ov_vi> (last accessed 9 March 2018).
2. On the benefits of having a Triune God (Father, Son and Holy Spirit), a helpful resource for me has been this three-part audio series: <https://www.theologynetwork.org/christian-beliefs/doctrine-of-god/enjoying-the-trinity-1-a-delightfully-different.htm> (last accessed 8 August 2018).
3. Lynda Brownback, *Finding God in My Loneliness* (Wheaton, IL: Crossway, 2017).
4. Hebrews 12:24 even points to greater grace, as his brother's blood crying out for judgment is soon silenced by the cry of the blood of Christ from the cross, answering all judgment and heaping grace after grace for those who trust him.

5. Thanks to D. A. Carson for this helpful phrase in *The God Who Is There* (Grand Rapids, MI: Baker Books, 2010).

6. One must be careful not to read things into history at this point. If we are aware of our history, we cannot draw any comparisons to modern-day east and west divisions. Throughout history it has not been true that God has always cast the east as negative.

7. S. Corbett and B. Fikkert, *When Helping Hurts* (Chicago, IL: Moody, 2014) and R. D. Lupton, *Toxic Charity* (New York: HarperOne, 2011).

8. Blaise Pascal, *Pensées* (Oxford: Oxford University Press, 2008).

9. Alexander Solzhenitsyn, *The Gulag Archipelago* (London: Harvill Press, 2003).

## 3. Travelling the world with new lenses

1. Robert Louis Stevenson, *The Silverado Squatters* (London: Tauris Parke Paperbacks, 2009).

2. To analyse what type of culture you are from, check out <www.theculturetest.com> (last accessed 10 March 2018).

3. Equally, some have tried to pin the difference in Western culture on Protestant (guilt–innocence) cultures and Roman Catholic (shame–honour) cultures. Although there are valid examples of this, it is probably too simplistic an understanding. Perhaps it would be better to look at what culture exists in Nonconformist church settings (i.e. where the denomination is not of the prevailing cultural or ruling ideology), and see whether the sociological values impact on what lens is adopted, thereby distancing religious difference.

4. You could think about political lenses – how does a left-wing person read the Bible differently from a right-wing person? Or you could think of it from a theological stance – how does an Arminian read Scripture differently from a Reformed person? If you're keen to explore more, there are some suggestions in the 'Recommended reading'.

5. N. Beynon, *Dig Deeper* (Nottingham: IVP, 2010); Vaughan Roberts, *God's Big Picture* (Leicester: IVP, 2003); J. Rhodes, *Raiding the Lost Ark* (Nottingham: IVP, 2013).

6. Augustine, *Letter* 43.

7. By this I mean those things the Bible speaks about a lot: for example, the need for a Saviour, our sinfulness, the person of Christ, his death and resurrection, the community of believers and life everlasting.

## 4. Home is where the heart is

1. Eric Roth, *The Curious Case of Benjamin Button* (directed by D. Fincher, 2009).

2. See 2 Chronicles 9 or 1 Kings 10.

3. Thanks to Timothy Keller for this neat phrase.

4. <www.unz.com/print/SaturdayRev-1974feb23-00025/> (last accessed 10 March 2018).

5. I can think of one big question this may raise for us: how continuous is the old covenant with the new covenant today? By that, I mean should we expect divine, travelling, raiding parties (or earthquakes, tsunamis and other such) to come sweeping across unfaithful nations today? Or, even if God doesn't relate so much to nations any more (and that's a question), is their correlation to individuals? Perhaps Luke 13 (the Tower of Siloam) and the death of Jesus could help us. I'm not sure ISIS or earthquakes are specific judgments necessarily (for God's divine justice will largely be satisfied at the cross or on judgment day), but as we do not know (God's wrath is being revealed continuously, according to Romans 1), let us turn from our sin and call others to do so regardless. May the catastrophes of this world keep us sharp in our spirituality.

## 5. To the nations! Where next?

1. <http://picoiyerjourneys.com/index.php/2000/03/why-we-travel/> (last accessed February 2018).

2. Ezekiel 47:1–12; 43:1–12; Isaiah 44:3; 55:1–3; Ezekiel 37:15–28.

3. Isaiah 49:6; 2:2–4; Genesis 12.

4. For further study, some fascinating questions of church history arise:

   • 'The blood of the martyrs is the seed of the Church' is often quoted, but where was this not true? Did the Church seemingly die out in places?

   • Why did the Reformation take off so well – what were the human circumstances building up to allow it to flourish?

   • The Jesuit (Roman Catholic) movement was one of the biggest migrations of missionaries in all of history, but how did they suddenly appear in vast numbers and reach the nations with their message when not a lot had happened before?

   • William Carey is often called the founder of the Protestant modern missionary movement in the last few centuries. What limited missionary travel took place before that?

   • More Muslims are said to be coming to Christ today than in all other centuries combined previously. Why might this be?

5. That is not to rule out those who philosophically adopt a Cartesian dualism, or indeed a non-Cartesian dualism. Frequently ridiculed in secular lecture halls, it bears a lot more consideration before being discarded.

6. Those tempted by this on the grounds that it gets more evangelism done quicker, I would encourage to consider there are far better ways to motivate evangelism theologically and keep a thriving and growing church scene than by demeaning other things in this world.

7. Paul's theology of preaching:
   - 2 Corinthians 4:4–6 – spiritual blindness
   - 2 Corinthians 5:11 – godly persuasion
   - 2 Corinthians 10:4–5 – divine demolition.
8. With thanks to Universities and Colleges Christian Fellowship's Christian Persuader programme for these headings.
9. Notably, there are other forms of travelling evangelism encountered very frequently in today's society, like finding 'people of peace' (justified by Luke 10), or simply uttering four-step gospel presentations, or handing out tracts or Gospels like sweets. Thankfully, God is gracious enough to use our weak efforts, but we'd do well to follow persuasive patterns like these.
10. Matthew 28:18–20; Mark 16:15–18; Luke 24:45–49; John 20:21–23; (Acts 1:8).
11. D. B. Barrett and T. M. Johnson, *World Christian Trends AD 30 – AD 2200: Interpreting the Annual Christian Megacensus*, associate eds., Christopher R. Guidry and Peter F. Crossing (Pasadena, CA: William Carey Library, 2001). M. R. Baxter, *The Coming Revolution: Because Status Quo Missions Won't Finish the Job* (Mustang, OK: Tate Publishing, 2007).

## 6. Dying to travel

1. Philippians 1:21.
2. J. A. Shedd, *Salt from My Attic* (Portland, MA: The Mosher Press, 1928).
3. Norman Grubb, *C. T. Studd: Cricketer and Pioneer* (Cambridge: Lutterworth Press, 1987). C. T. Studd was an English international cricketer, famously one of the 'Cambridge Seven', who left to be a missionary in China. The stories of all seven can be found in John Pollock, *The Cambridge Seven* (Tain: Christian Focus, 2012).
4. F. and L. Chan, *You and Me Forever* (Claire Love Publishing, 2014).

5. With thanks for this phrase to Dick Brogden and others at <www.livedead.org> (last accessed 11 March 2018).

## 7. Made for better travel

1. C. S. Lewis, *Letters to an American Lady* (Grand Rapids, MI: Eerdmans, 2014).
2. G. K. Chesterton, *The Victorian Age in Literature* (Fairford: Echo Library, 2008).
3. Evelyn Waugh, *When the Going Was Good* (London: Penguin, 2011).
4. N. Guthrie, *Even Better than Eden* (Wheaton, IL: Crossway, 2018).
5. Christendom – where Jesus' spiritual goals got caught up with institutionalizing a religion into the main framework of politics and culture, giving it special privilege.
6. *Tao Te Ching* ('The Book of the Way').
7. C. S. Lewis, *The Weight of Glory and Other Addresses*, ed. Walter Hooper (New York: Simon & Schuster, 1996), pp. 25–6.
8. C. S. Lewis, *Mere Christianity* (New York: HarperCollins, 2001), p. 137.
9. A. Camus, *The Fall*, in *Plague, Fall, Exile and The Kingdom and Selected Essays* (New York: Everyman, 2004).
10. Homer, *Odyssey* XII.

# RECOMMENDED READING

For more insights on each chapter and multimedia content that goes alongside each chapter, please go online to <https://aljabr7.wordpress.com/book/>.

**Faith and travel (general)**

Nicki Jeffery, *Faith-based Travels: A Devotional Guidebook for the Faith-filled Traveller* (Port Orchard, WA: Ark House Press, 2015)

Stephen Liggins, *Travelling the World as Citizens of Heaven* (Waterloo, NSW: Matthias Media, 2017)

Joerg Rieger, *Faith on the Road: A Short Theology of Travel and Justice* (Downers Grove, IL: IVP, 2016)

Kevin Wright, *The Christian Travel Planner* (Nashville, TN: Thomas Nelson, 2012)

**1. In the land of the Midnight Sun**

Julian Hardyman, *Maximum Life: All for the Glory of God* (Nottingham: IVP, 2009)

Timothy Keller, 'A Biblical Theology of the City', <https://mustardseedkingdom.wordpress.com/2013/07/30/tim-keller-on-a-biblical-theology-of-the-city/> (last accessed 12 July 2018)

John Lennox, *Seven Days that Divide the World: The Beginning according to Genesis and Science* (Grand Rapids, MI: Zondervan, 2011)

Michael Reeves, *The Good God: Enjoying Father, Son and Spirit* (Milton Keynes: Paternoster Press, 2012)

## 2. Travelling east of Eden

Lydia Brownback, *Finding God in My Loneliness* (Wheaton, IL: Crossway, 2017)

## 3. Travelling the world with new lenses

Nigel Beynon and Andrew Sach, *Dig Deeper: Tools to Unearth the Bible's Treasure* (Nottingham: IVP, 2010)

Jayson Georges and Mark D. Baker, *Ministering in Honor-Shame Cultures: Biblical Foundations and Practical Essentials* (Downers Grove, IL: IVP, 2017)

Jonty Rhodes, *Raiding the Lost Ark: Recovering the Gospel of the Covenant King* (Nottingham: IVP, 2013)

Vaughan Roberts, *God's Big Picture* (Nottingham: IVP, 2009)

Carl R. Trueman, *Republocrat: Confessions of a Liberal Conservative* (Phillipsburg, NJ: P&R, 2012)

## 4. Home is where the heart is

Andrew Sach and Richard Alldritt, *Dig Even Deeper* (Nottingham: IVP, 2011)

Chris Sinkinson, *Time Travel to the Old Testament* (Nottingham: IVP, 2013)

## 5. To the nations! Where next?

Richard Cunningham (ed.), *Serving the Church, Reaching the World: Essays in Honour of Don Carson* (London: IVP, 2017)

William Edgar, *Reasons of the Heart: Recovering Christian Persuasion* (Phillipsburg, NJ: P&R, 2012)

Jason Mandryk, *Operation World: The Definitive Prayer Guide to Every Nation* (Downers Grove, IL: IVP, 2012)

John G. Paton, *John G Paton: Missionary to the New Hebrides – An Autobiography* (London: Forgotten Books, 2012)

John Piper and David Mathis, *Finish the Mission: Bringing the Gospel to the Unreached and Unengaged* (Wheaton, IL: Crossway, 2012)

## 6. Dying to travel/7. Made for better travel

Dick Brogden, *Live Dead Journal: 30 Days of Prayer for Unreached Peoples, 30 Days of Challenge* (Akron, OH: University of Akron Press, 2012)

Tim Chester and Steve Timmis, *Everyday Church: Mission by Being Good Neighbours* (Nottingham: IVP, 2011)

Tim Chester and Steve Timmis, *Total Church: A Radical Reshaping around Gospel and Community* (Nottingham, IVP: 2007)

Edward Donnelly, *Heaven and Hell* (Edinburgh: Banner of Truth, 2001)

Mark Greene, *Thank God it's Monday: Ministry in the Workplace* (Milton Keynes: Scripture Union, 2001)

Michael S. Horton, *Ordinary* (Grand Rapids, MI: Zondervan, 2014)

C. S. Lewis, *Mere Christianity* (London: HarperCollins, 2012)

C. S. Lewis, *Surprised by Joy* (London: HarperCollins, 2012)

C. S. Lewis, *The Weight of Glory: A Collection of Lewis' Most Moving Addresses* (London: HarperCollins, 2013) John Piper, *Don't Waste Your Life* (Wheaton, IL: Crossway, 2018)

David Platt, *Radical: Taking Back Your Faith from the American Dream* (Colorado Springs, CO: Multnomah Books, 2010)